A
STYLE MANUAL
FOR
WRITTEN COMMUNICATION

by

Arno F. Knapper, Ph.D.
School of Business
University of Kansas

and

Loda I. Newcomb, M.S.
School of Education
University of Kansas

Fifth Printing

INTRODUCTION

In this style manual the authors have attempted to give a straightforward presentation of correct, acceptable usage and style without lengthy discussions of semantics, word derivations, and pros and cons of acceptable usage and style.

Writers may have two objectives when writing — communication and/or self-expression. This manual has been prepared for writers whose objective is communication. These writers should be concerned with getting ideas into the minds of readers without misunderstanding and without interruption of thought. They should not be interested primarily in self-expression because they are writing for the convenience and the benefit of readers, not for self-benefit. Therefore, for writers whose objective is communication, the authors recommend and urge the use of traditionally acceptable English that has stood the test of understandable communication.

The authors have taken the point of view that readers who know the traditionally correct language may be distracted or even offended by incorrect usage, though generally accepted, while readers who do not know the traditionally correct language will be neither distracted nor offended. The authors gladly accept the criticism of those who know the traditionally correct language and feel it should give way to more common usage.

In writing this manual, the authors clearly recognized that they stood decidedly in favor of traditionally correct English usage. Some English instructors may well consider that the authors have taken a step backward in the evolution of acceptable usage of the English language. Be that as it may, the authors do look with favor on changes in acceptable usage if the changes have purpose; but they see no reason for changing traditionally good language unless changes improve expression and communication. Written language should be used to communicate ideas, not to attract attention to the language or simply to get something off the mind of the writer. "Sidewalk" expressions, words, and phrases used in writing may bring criticism and, consequently, distract the reader from the intended meaning of context. This book is designed to help the writer achieve his intended meaning.

AFK and LIN

TABLE OF CONTENTS

LETTER MECHANICS

Letters serve as personal envoys to correspondents. The impression a letter creates is the impression the reader gets of the writer of the letter.

The following pages present several styles of letters and explain the various parts of a letter.

Letter styles

Pages 2 through 6 present five styles of business letters:

1. Block, page 2
2. Simplified, page 3
3. Modified block, page 4
4. Indented, page 5
5. Official, page 6

The contexts of the letters describe the distinctive features of each style of letter.

Styles of letter punctuation

The sample letters on pages 2, 4, and 5 illustrate three styles of letter punctuation:

1. Open, page 2
2. Mixed, page 4, 6
3. Closed, page 5

The special features of each style of punctuation are explained in the individual letters.

Letterheads

Letterheads should contain three vital pieces of information: (1) Who you are, (2) What you are, and (3) Where you are. Telephone numbers and area code numbers, as well as Zip Code numbers, should be printed in the letterhead.

For stationery without a printed letterhead, the writer's return address is typed ten to twelve spaces from the top edge of the stationery and is started at the middle of the page or at the left margin, depending upon the style of letter used.

Example: 1604 University Drive
Aspen, Colorado 81611

July 1, 1974

LETTERHEAD

July 1, 1974

The ABC Company
1234 56th Street S.E.
Havre, Montana 59501

Gentlemen

This is a block style of letter and is so named because all lines
are blocked at the left margin.

Although this style of letter is not often used, it has at least
one feature that makes it popular among secretaries. Because all
lines are blocked at the left margin, considerable time is saved
in typing this style of letter.

Since the block style is rather infrequently used, it appears
rather severe and impersonal to a reader who is not accustomed
to seeing it. Although severe styles may attract attention,
they may also distract the reader from the message of the letter.

This letter also illustrates the open style of punctuation. In
this style no punctuation marks appear after the date, the lines
of the inside address (except after the abbreviation), the salutation,
the complimentary close, and the signature line.

In recent years the block style with open punctuation has become
increasingly popular.

Sincerely yours

Roger L. Brown

Roger L. Brown
Office Manager

fl

(Block Style - Open Punctuation)

L E T T E R H E A D

July 1, 1974

Mr. Craig Blair, Office Manager
The XYZ Company
1234 Modern Avenue
Cleveland, Ohio 44100

THE SIMPLIFIED LETTER STYLE

This letter is typed in the simplified style, a modification
of the block style.

The simplified style is distinguished by the absence of
the salutation and the complimentary close. When subject
lines are used, subject is omitted; and the description
is typed in capital letters.

Although many people and some organizations advocate using
the simplified style because of its simplicity, the style has
been slow to gain popularity.

Larry Johnson

LARRY JOHNSON – OFFICE MANAGER

ad

(Simplified Style - Open Punctuation)

LETTERHEAD

July 1, 1974

Mr. John P. Johnson, C.P.A.
Arthur Thompsen and Company
543 Equitable Building
One Grand Avenue
Kansas City, Missouri   64100

Dear Mr. Johnson:

Subject: Letter Styles

This letter is an example of the modified-block style. All lines of
the letter are blocked at the left margin except the date, the subject
line, the complimentary close, and the signature line. Often the
modified block is varied slightly by indenting the first line of each
paragraph.

* Examples of five other styles of letters are enclosed. However, the
modified-block style is perhaps the most popular style of letter used
in business.

The asterisks in the left margin are reminders to the stenographer
and to the reader that the letter has enclosures. Many stenographers
have been embarrassed by forgetting enclosures, and many readers
have been annoyed because stenographers have forgotten enclosures.

This letter illustrates the mixed style of punctuation. In this style
a colon is used after the salutation, and a comma is placed after the
complimentary close. Mixed punctuation is probably the most frequently
used style of letter punctuation.

Because the modified-block style is so frequently used in business, a
writer can be confident that the modified-block style with either blocked
or indented paragraphs will be acceptable to his reader.

Cordially yours,

Donald A. Keller
Office Manager

fl

* Enclosures

(Modified-block Style - Mixed Punctuation)

L E T T E R H E A D

July 1, 1974

Mr. John P. Quigley,
    523 West Elm Street,
        Bangor, Maine 04401

Dear Mr. Quigley:

This letter is typed in the indented style. The first line of the inside address is typed at the left margin, and each succeeding line is indented five spaces under the preceding line.

The salutation is typed at the left margin, and the first line of each paragraph is indented. The complimentary close begins slightly left of the center of the page; the signature line and each additional line is indented.

Closed-punctuation style is used in this letter. In this style a period is placed after the date, and commas are placed after each line of the inside address except the last line, where a period is used. A colon is placed after the salutation, a comma after the complimentary close, a comma after the signature line, and a period after the title.

The indented style and closed punctuation are virtually unused in modern business correspondence. Many years ago these styles were perhaps the most frequently used styles in business correspondence. Today they are considered old fashioned.

Sincerely yours,

Walter L. Primrose,
Office Manager.

ss

(Indented Style - Closed Punctuation)

LETTERHEAD

July 1, 1974

Dear Mrs. Reed:

This letter illustrates the official style of letters
that is used extensively for three specific types of letters.

First, as the name implies, this style is used for
messages of an official nature. Second, it is used for
formal messages to people of high position. Third, it is
used for nonbusiness messages to people who are not known
by the writer. Some companies, however, are extending its
use to regular day-to-day business matters.

Most noteworthy of the official style is the placement
of the inside address four to six lines below the reference
notation.

Very sincerely yours,

Albert J. Washburn

op

Mrs. Elizabeth M. Reed
6500 Pine Bluff Parkway
Valley City, North Dakota 58072

(Official Style - Mixed Punctuation)

Placement of letters

There are many complicated ways to determine the placement of a letter on a page. However, the experienced typist places a letter by judgment. The typist's objective is to place the letter so that the right, left, and bottom margins are of approximately equal size. The sample letters illustrated on the preceding pages were placed by judgment.

The letter chart appearing on this page shows the length of type-written line to use for short, medium, and long letters. If a letter contains tabulated material, more space should be planned on the page for the letter.

LETTER-PLACEMENT CHART

Length of Letter	First Line of Inside Address	Spaces in Typewritten Line	
		Elite Type (12 spaces to inch)	Pica Type (10 spaces to inch)
Short (Up to 100 words)	22-24	50	40
Medium (100 to 200 words)	20-22	60	50
Long (200 to 300 words)	17-20	70	60
Two pages (over 300 words)	17-20	70	60
Type the dateline two spaces below the last line in the letterhead.			

Dateline

Every letter should be dated. Dates should never be abbreviated, nor should numbers be used for months.

Examples: December 21, 1974
31 December 1974 (military style)

Inside address

1.   Every address should contain at least three lines. If only the name, city, state, and Zip Code are needed for prompt delivery, place them on three lines at the left margin.

Example: Mr. John Jones
Revere
Minnesota 56166

2. Use abbreviations sparingly. Do not abbreviate *street, avenue, place, road, boulevard, terrace, court,* and *building* or cities, names, and directions. Spell out street names that are numbers from first through tenth, but use figures for street names above ten.

(See abbreviations of states and territories, p. 94.)

Examples: Mr. John P. Jones, Attorney
           623 Fidelity Building
           8326 South Third Street
           Philadelphia, Pennsylvania 19100

           The Cultural Society
           1624 Avenue J, N.W.
           Washington, D.C. 20000

(Note: *Northwest, Northeast, Southwest,* and *Southeast* are abbreviated only when they are placed at the end of the street addresses.)

3. Do not use redundant titles (e.g., Dr. James Smith, M.D.)

Attention line

The attention line is typed a double space below the city and the state and a double space above the salutation. It may begin at the left margin, be indented from the left margin, or be centered horizontally on the page. *Attention* is often followed by a colon.

Examples: Attention: Mr. John Jones, Personnel Manager
           Attention of Mr. John Jones, Personnel Manager

Salutation

The salutation is written at the left margin, a double space under the inside address. It should always agree with the first line of the inside address. If the first line of the address is the name of a company, *Gentlemen* should be used as a salutation even though a person's name is given in an attention line. (See "Complimentary close," p. 9, for the appropriate matching of salutations with complimentary closes.)

Subject line

A subject line, when used, is a double space below the salutation and a double space above the first paragraph of the body of the letter. It may be centered horizontally or placed at the left margin. *Subject* is often indented and is followed by a colon. *Re* and *In re* are obsolete substitutes for *Subject.*

Example: Subject: Placement of subject lines

Body

Paragraphs in the body of a letter should be single-spaced, but double spacing should be used between paragraphs. Keep paragraphs short—seldom more than six lines. On the other hand, do not overparagraph.

Complimentary close

Capitalize only the first letter of the first word of a complimentary close. Unless the block style is used, begin the complimentary close near the horizontal center of the page and a double space below the body of the letter.

The complimentary close should be of the same degree of formality as the salutation:

	(Sir (or) Madam	(Respectfully yours
	(My dear Sir	(Yours respectfully
	(My dear Madam	(Yours truly
Formal	(Dear Sir (or) Dear Madam	(Very truly yours
	(My dear Mr. Jones	(Yours very truly
	(My dear Mrs. Jones	(
	(	(Yours sincerely
	(Ladies	(Yours cordially
	(Gentlemen	(Sincerely yours
Informal	(Ladies and Gentlemen	(Cordially yours
	(Gentlemen	(Sincerely
	(Dear Mr. Jones	(Cordially
	(Dear Ms. Smith	(
Personal	(Dear Jim	(Sincerely
	(	(Cordially

Second-page heading

Although two-page letters are infrequent, second pages, which are typed on plain sheets of bond paper, should be labeled to provide identification in case the pages are separated. The identification containing the name of the addressee, the page number, and the date should be typed about an inch and a half from the top of the second page. A triple space is left between the heading and the body of the letter. Never use a second page for only one line of a paragraph or for just the complimentary close and signature line.

The bottom margin on the first page of a two-page letter should be approximately the same width as the side margins.

Examples: Mr. John J. Jones
              Page 2
              July 1, 1974

July 1, 1974

Company name

When the company name is printed on the letterhead, it need not be written after the complimentary close; however, if it is not on the letterhead, it may be typed in capital letters a double space below the complimentary close.

Example: Sincerely yours

THE ABC COMPANY

Signature line

A typed signature line should be placed about four spaces below the complimentary close or the company name. The signature line may be omitted if the writer's name is on the letterhead or if the signature is easily read. Women frequently indicate their marital status in the signature line. If a woman chooses not to indicate her marital status and if her name does not clearly indicate that she is a woman, she should use *Ms.* as an abbreviation for *Miss* or *Mrs. Mr.* is never typed in the signature line but is assumed as the appropriate title if *Ms., Miss,* or *Mrs.* is not indicated.

Examples: Sincerely yours   Sincerely yours

Bessie Brown   *John J. Smith*
Mrs. Bessie Brown   John J. Smith
                                   Office Manager

Sincerely yours   Sincerely yours

                                   THE ABC COMPANY

Bessie Brown   *John Q. Doe*
Bessie Brown   John Q. Doe
(Mrs. A. B. Brown)   Sales Representative

Sincerely yours   Sincerely

Sylvia Smith   *Lynn Jones*
Miss Sylvia Smith   Lynn Jones

Sincerely yours   Sincerely yours

Sylvia Smith   *Lynn Jones*
Sylvia Smith   Ms. Lynn Jones

Reference notation

1. The dictator's initials need not be typed in the reference notation unless the dictator is someone other than the person who signs the letter. When the dictator's initials are typed, they are separated from the stenographer's initials by a colon or a diagonal. Occasionally, when a signature line is not typed, the signer's name is placed in the reference notation. If no signature line is typed, four to six vertical spaces should be left between the complimentary close and the reference initials.

Examples: fl
            PLK:fl (or) PLK/fl
            PaulLKelly:fl
            Paul L. Kelly:fl

2. Enclosures, distribution of copies, and special mailing notations are placed below the reference initials. These notations may be single- or double-spaced, depending upon the space available for them.

Examples: fl
            Enclosure
            Copies to: J. B. Jones
                       Charles R. Buck
            Registered Air Mail

            fl
            Enclosures: 1. Check for $5
                         2. Application form

            Manuscript in separate envelope

3. An asterisk may be placed in the left margin of the body of the letter where an enclosure is mentioned. A second asterisk is then placed in the margin by the enclosure notation. These asterisks remind the typist to enclose the materials referred to and also remind the reader of the enclosures. (See sample letter on page 4.)

4. A blind carbon-copy notation may be typed in the upper-left corner of the carbon copy to be filed. The notation should not appear on the original copy, hence the name "blind."

Postscripts

Postscripts are obviously postscripts and need not be labeled *P.S.* They are typed a double space under the last item of the reference notation.

Envelopes

1. Envelope addresses should be identical to inside addresses both in content and in style. Three-line addresses should be double-spaced.

Addresses of more than three lines are single-spaced. Start the address at the midpoint, both vertically and horizontally, of the envelope. Names of cities must be spelled in full, and "City" should never be substituted for the name of a city or a town since mail is often sorted in cities other than where it is deposited.

2.   Attention lines, with all important words capitalized, are placed on the second line of an envelope address or in the lower-left corner of the envelope.

3.   Special mailing notations in capital letters should be placed below the stamp.

4.   If the envelope does not have a printed return address, the sender's name and address should be typed in the upper-left corner.

Example:

```
XYZ Metal Company
1509 Concord Avenue
Detroit, Michigan  48200                    AIR MAIL


                        The ABC Company

                        321 West 65th Street

                        Dover, Delaware  19901

Attention: Personnel Manager
```

Folding of letters

Large envelope. To fold a letter to be inserted in a large (Nos. 7 3/4, 9, 10) envelope, use the following method:

1. Place the letter on the desk with the face up.
2. Fold the bottom edge up slightly less than one third of the page.
3. Fold the top edge down, leaving about one-half inch at the bottom of the first fold.
4. Insert the letter into the envelope with the top of the letter at the top edge of the envelope and with the face of the letter toward you.

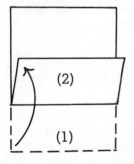
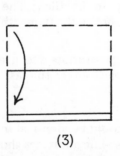
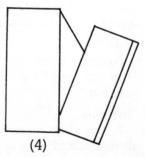

Small envelope. To fold a letter to be inserted in a small (Nos. 6 1/4 and 6 3/4) envelope, use the following method:

1. Place the letter on the desk with the face up.
2. Fold the bottom edge up to one-half inch from the top edge of the paper.
3. Fold the right third of the letter to the left.
4. Fold the left third of the letter to the right, leaving about one-half inch of the right edge showing.
5. Insert the letter into the envelope with the last fold going inside the envelope first.

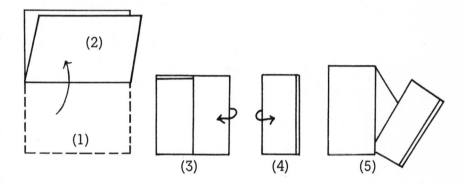

Window envelope. To fold a letter to be inserted into a window envelope, use the following method:

1. Place the letter on the desk with the face up.
2. Fold the bottom edge of the letter up about one third of the sheet of paper.
3. Fold the top edge of the letter back to the first fold so that the inside address will be visible.
4. Insert the letter into the envelope with the address toward the front of the envelope.

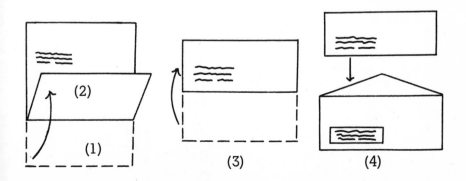

REPORT MECHANICS

Written reports are becoming an increasingly important means of communication in American society. In business, for example, seldom is an activity accomplished without a written report concerning it.

Reports may vary from a full-blown report of original research to a one- or two-sentence memorandum. Yet, regardless of size or nature, all reports have one pervading characteristic — they are communications of useful information from one person or one group to another person or another group. This characteristic, then, sets the stage for the preparation of any report: A report must be prepared for the convenience and the purpose of the reader, for it is the reader who uses the information presented in a report.

In the following pages mechanics of report preparation are presented. The presentation is limited, however, to typewritten reports. Printed books and monographs may very well be considered reports; and the writers of such reports should consult cartographers, artists, printers, and other professionals concerning diagrams, drawings, typesettings, and other mechanical devices that may be used.

Outline

An outline is a valuable aid in the organization of thoughts and can save much time and effort in writing a report.

Capital Roman numerals are used for major headings. The first subdivisions are introduced by capital letters. The next subdivisions are indicated by Arabic numerals. The breakdowns under the Arabic numerals are marked by lower-case letters. If an additional division is desired, small Roman numerals are used. Parentheses are frequently placed around the subdivision letters and numerals, and the periods following the letters and numerals are omitted.

Example: I. — — — — — — — — — —
             A. — — — — — — — — — —
                1. — — — — — — — — — —
                   a. — — — — — — — — — —
                     i. — — — — — — — — — —
                    ii. — — — — — — — — — —
                   b. — — — — — — — — — —
                2. — — — — — — — — — —
             B. — — — — — — — — — —
          II. — — — — — — — — — —

An outline may consist of topics, sentences, or, rarely, paragraphs. The topic outline is most frequently used. Parallel structure must be maintained throughout the outline. (See "Parallel structure," under "Grammar Problems," p. 62.) When a topic is divided, two divisions result; that is, if "A" is used, "B" must also be used. If "1" is used, at least "2" must follow.

Indent all subdivisions so that the introductory number or letter begins under the first letter of the preceding item. All numerals and letters must line at the right side within their respective divisions.

If the topic is short, no punctuation is needed at the end of the line; if the item is long, a period may be used. Capitalize only the first word of each item unless a proper noun is in the item.

The following outline presents the parts of a full-blown research report. Any given report indeed may include only a portion of or may be an abbreviated adaptation of a full-blown report. Subdivisions of the outline may be combined, eliminated, modified, or rearranged for appropriateness of presentation.

   I. Introductory material
      A. Title page
      B. Letter of transmittal, acknowledgments, preface, or foreword
      C. Abstract or summary
      D. Contents
      E. List or table of tables
      F. List of illustrations, charts, figures, or graphs

  II. Body
      A. Introduction
         1. Introductory statement
         2. Statement of problem
         3. Importance of problem
         4. Statement of purpose
         5. Definition of scope
         6. Statement of limitations
      B. Historical background
         1. Review of literature
         2. Review of theory
         3. Definitions of terms
         4. Procedure of research
         5. Organization of the study
      C. Text—presentation and analysis
         (The outline would be expanded according to the logical division of the presentation and analysis.)
      D. Summary of research
      E. Conclusions
      F. Recommendations

 III. Appendix (supplementary tables, graphs, questionnaires, checklists, methods of computation, calculations, etc.)

    IV. Exhibits (photographs, reproductions, and samples)
    V. Bibliography
    VI. Index

Pagination

Introductory pages are numbered in lower-case Roman numerals. The title page is assigned Roman "i" although the number need not be typed. For other preliminary pages a lower-case Roman numeral is centered horizontally one inch above the bottom edge of the page.

Arabic numbers are used in the body and on all succeeding pages of the report, including the appendix, bibliography, and index.

The pages of the body of a report may be numbered in any of three places. The first and preferred place is the upper-right corner one inch down from the top edge and one inch in from the right edge of the paper. Page numbers may be centered either one inch down from the top edge of the page or one inch up from the bottom edge. A triple space is left between the last line typed and the number when the page number is centered at the bottom of the page.

The first page of the body of a report is assigned Arabic "1" although the numeral need not be typed. The first page of each chapter is also assigned a number although that number need not be typed.

Format

The first concern in selecting an appropriate format for a report is how the format will contribute to readability. Certainly a dark typewriter ribbon and high-quality bond paper, size 8½ by 11 inches, should be used. Typing is done only on one side of a page.

A report may be bound or stapled at the left, at the top, or at the upper-left corner. The report should be attractive enough to invite the reader's attention to it and make him want to read it. The attractiveness of a report will add a great deal to the authority and the confidence the reader places in the report.

Title page. The title page should contain the following information arranged in a logical, attractive order:

1. Title of the report (in upper-case letters)
2. Author's name
3. Brief statement of purpose if not included in the title
4. Name of person for whom the report is prepared
5. Date

Pages 18 and 19 are sample title pages. The title is typed in upper-case letters about two inches from the top edge of the page, and at least a one-inch margin is left at the bottom of the page.

Letter of transmittal or acknowledgment. If a letter of transmittal is used in a report, the letter would be prepared like any letter prepared for mailing. The letter should be off center to the right if

THE USEFULNESS OF PREDICTING FUTURE SALES

FROM EMPLOYMENT-TEST SCORES

A Correlation Analysis

for

Mr. Earle R. Smithson
Director of Personnel
ABC Corporation

by

Frank Lynn
Personnel Assistant

Submitted as a suggestion
on personnel procedures

July 1, 1974

(Sample Title Page)

THE USEFULNESS
OF PREDICTING FUTURE SALES
FROM EMPLOYMENT-TEST SCORES
(A Correlation Analysis)

for

Mr. Earl R. Smithson
Director of Personnel
ABC Corporation

by

Frank Lynn
Personnel Assistant

Submitted as a suggestion
on personnel procedures

July 1, 1974

(Sample Title Page)

the report is bound at the left margin, and the margins of the letter should not be less than an inch and a half on the left and one inch on the right and at the bottom.

An acknowledgment page is double spaced and placed slightly to the right of the center of the page. "Acknowledgments" is typed in upper-case letters. (See the example on page 21.)

Abstract or summary. The same format used in the body of the report is used in the abstract.

Contents. The contents page and all other introductory tables are typed in the same format. (See example, page 22.) The titles of tables are typed in upper-case letters about an inch and a half from the top edge of the paper. Leave a triple space after the title before the first entry. Double spacing should usually be used except for second-level subdivisions, which are single spaced. Too much single-spaced material makes reading difficult. Chapter headings are typed in capital letters. For reports stapled at the left or at the upper-left corner, one inch is allowed for the right margin, one inch for the bottom margin, and an inch and a half for the left margin. For reports stapled at the top, the top margin is enlarged for binding; and one inch is allowed for each of the side and bottom margins. If the table of contents is only a partial page, the bottom margin is enlarged accordingly.

Type *Chapter* or *Heading* at the left margin and type *Page* so that "e" ends at the right margin. The Arabic numerals placed under the heading should align so that the last digit ends at the right margin. Each chapter Roman numeral has a period following it, and numerals always line at the right.

The items listed on the contents page are typed in the same style used in the body of the report; and the items include all chapter, division, and subdivision titles in the report. Letters or numbers starting the headings or subheadings are indented under the preceding heading. If more than one line is needed for a heading, the second line is indented two spaces more than the first line.

Leaders (periods separated by spaces) are used to guide the reader from the listings to the appropriate page numbers. To assure vertical alignment of the leaders, check to see whether the first line of leaders is typed on odd or even spaces; then type the succeeding lines by starting all of them on odd numbers or all of them on even numbers. Only the last line of a multiple-line item is followed by leaders. Leaders should start about two or three spaces after each topic and extend to about two or three spaces before the longest page number. All lines of leaders should stop at the same point on the right side.

Body. For a report exceeding two pages, the body is usually double spaced but may be single spaced provided the paragraphs and subdivisions are short enough to give plenty of "white space." Nothing is

ACKNOWLEDGMENTS

The author of this study is deeply indebted to the eighty-nine salesmen who directly participated in the study and to the personnel and statistical clerks who helped gather and process the data.

Special appreciation is extended to Mr. George Fox, Chief Statistician, for his guidance and helpful comments regarding the design of the statistical analysis.

Without the generous cooperation of these people this study would not have been possible.

(Sample Acknowledgment Page)

CONTENTS

(Sample Table of Contents)

(Sample Table of Contents)

more discouraging to a reader than long, black paragraphs of single-spaced typewriting. Double-spaced paragraphs must be indented, usually five spaces. Page 24 presents the first page of a typewritten report that illustrates the format of the body.

In a report not divided into chapters or sections, the title of the report, typed in upper-case letters, is placed two inches from the top edge of the first page of the body. A triple space is left between the report title and the first line of context.

In a report divided into chapters, *Chapter* and its number, with only the "C" and the Roman numeral in upper-case letters, are typed two inches from the top edge of the page. A double space is left between this line and the chapter title.

The title of a chapter or a major division is typed a double space below the chapter number. If more than one line is needed for a title, single-space between the lines and divide the title so that each succeeding line is shorter than the preceding one, keeping all words in a phrase together if possible. Begin the first line of the text a triple space after the title.

One and a half inches are allowed for the left margin and one inch each for the right and bottom margins. The first line of context of all pages succeeding the page on which the chapter title is typed is begun a double or a triple space below the page number. If pages are numbered at the bottom, the first line of context should be at least an inch from the top edge of the paper.

Always be sure to have at least two lines of a paragraph at the bottom of a page and two lines at the top of a page. If a paragraph has only three lines, all three lines should be placed on the same page.

Long quotations (four lines or more) are indented five spaces from the right and the left margins and single-spaced with double spacing between paragraphs. No quotation marks are used for long quotations handled in this style. When a paragraph is omitted from quoted material, three asterisks with spaces between them are typed in the center of the page with a double space above the asterisks and a double space below them.

Appendix. Many forms and styles of presentation may be used in an appendix, yet the margins should be consistent with the margins in the body of the report.

Usually, separate the body of the report and the appendix by inserting one page with *appendix* or *appendixes* typed in upper-case letters in the center of the page. When more than one appendix is used, they are lettered in upper-case letters, e.g., APPENDIX A, APPENDIX B, and so forth. Frequently these separation pages contain listings of items placed in each appendix.

Exhibits. Exhibits are handled the same as appendixes.

Chapter I

INTRODUCTION

The Personnel Department of the ABC Corporation is charged with the responsibility of selecting and training salesmen. To select the best potential salesmen, the Department has used many devices for determining the qualifications of applicants for sales positions. The success of the Department depends upon how well the Department is able to predict the success of the salesmen it hires.

Personnel Testing and Sales Performance

One measure of the success of a salesman is determined by how much he sells after he is placed on the job. If the Personnel Department is to be successful, then it must be able to predict with some accuracy the volume of sales a salesman will produce. One method of prediction is the determination of the relationship between employment-test scores and sales volume.

If there is a reliable relationship between the score an applicant makes on a test and his sales record, then the test is useful in the selection of potentially successful salesmen.

Statement of the Problem

For many years the Personnel Department of the ABC Corporation has been testing applicants for sales positions. If the applicants scored high on the test and if other selection techniques appeared satisfactory, the applicants were offered

1

(Sample Report Page)

sales positions; however, no evidence has been obtained to determine whether the test scores were in any way helpful in selecting salesmen. The Department has been operating on the assumption that, if an applicant scores well on the test, he shows promise of becoming a good salesman. However, the Department does not know with any degree of confidence that an applicant with a high score will be a successful salesman.

While the testing program has been in effect, many applicants have succeeded as salesmen; others have failed. Has the testing been useful? If it has, how useful has it been? How much confidence can be placed in the scores? If the test has not been useful, what has been the purpose of giving the test?

Purpose of the Study

Because the company has been spending money on the testing program and has been taking the valuable time of applicants, there is need to determine whether such time and money are well spent. This study, then, is designed to determine three things:

1. Is the testing program a useful selection tool?
2. Does the test predict success or failure of an applicant?
3. What degree of confidence can be placed on test scores?

Definitions of Terms

If quantitative data (test scores and sales volume) are to have generalized meaning, they must be analyzed for significant relationships. Quantitative data may be added, subtracted, multiplied, and divided; they may be placed in arrays to show how they range from one extreme to another; they may be

2

(Sample Report Page)

Bibliography. The format for typing a bibliography is the same as that for appendixes. See "Bibliography," page 32, for details of presentation.

Index. As are all other parts of a report, the index is entirely for the use of the reader. Therefore, in constructing an index, the writer's foremost objective is to decide how a reader might use it. Is he likely to check the index for the names of people, names of products, geographical areas, subject matter, words and combinations of words related to subject matter, or any other classification of topics? Occasionally more than one index is constructed if frequent reference to a class of topics is expected. For example, if a reader is likely to check an index for authors' names at one time and for subject topics at another time, then two indexes may be useful.

Items a reader is likely to search for in an index are listed in alphabetical order. To facilitate alphabetizing the items, read through the report and record each item, as well as its page number, on a slip of paper or a 3 x 5 card. Then alphabetize the slips of paper and type the items. Often one subject may have several subdivisions. If so, indent the subdivisions about two spaces from the left margin. For example:

Apples
  Delicious
  Jonathan
  Tansparent
  Winesap

Headings

Headings (center-page, marginal, and paragraph) are perhaps the most valuable devices that can be used to promote the readability of a report. The reader can glance through a report, read only the headings, and obtain an overview of the organization and perspective of a complete report. Headings also prepare the reader for the content following a heading, and headings provide transition from one section of a report to another with minimum words. Triple-space before all headings except the chapter headings and double-space after them.

In typewritten copy there are three common positions for placing headings: center of the page, left margin, and first line of paragraph. For example, in a report entitled "Economic Development," the following headings may be used:

Potential Growth of Manufacturing

Contributions to growth
  Human resources. The . . .
  Higher education. The . . .

<u>Stable government</u>. The . . .

<u>Barriers to growth</u>
   <u>Taxes</u>. The . . .
   <u>Transportation</u>. The . . . .
   <u>Capital</u>. The . . .

<u>Potential Growth of Retailing</u>

* * *

Of course, all three positions may be used; or only one or two positions may be used; but the level of breakdown and the logical division of subject determine the number of positions used.

The wording of headings must be parallel, and the headings must be of the same level of abstraction. In the example, "Potential Growth of Manufacturing" and "Potential Growth of Retailing" have the same grammatical construction and the same level of abstractions from "Economic Development." "Contributions to growth" is parallel to and is of the same level of abstraction as "Barriers to growth." The same things are true for "Human resources," "Higher education," and "Stable government."

Headings are underscored to make them stand out from the context. At least the first letter of the first word of a heading is capitalized, and other important words in a heading may be capitalized; however, the same style of capitalization should be used for each heading position. In the example the important words in the center headings are capitalized, but only the first words are capitalized in the marginal and paragraph headings. Punctuation, a period, follows only paragraph headings. After the period, two spaces should be left.

Indeed, there may be intervening paragraphs that do not have paragraph headings; and in such cases the intervening paragraphs would be a part of the subject matter described by the preceding paragraph heading.

The first word or first few words of a paragraph may serve as a paragraph heading.

Examples: <u>Human resources</u> are important . . . .
               <u>Higher education</u> will promote . . . .
               <u>Stable government</u> enables businessmen . . .

Listings

Itemized listings may be set up with each item starting a new paragraph or set up with the numbers of the items to the left of the items.

Examples: 1. –
– –

or

1. – – – – – – – – – – – – – – – – – – –
– – – – – – – – – – – – – – – – – –

Footnotes

Footnotes may be of two types: (1) explanatory and (2) referential. Explanatory footnotes give additional explanation of the textual subject or incidental comment related to the textual subject. Referential footnotes refer the reader to a specific document.

In either type, footnotes are referred to by raised numbers or by asterisks, daggers, or other symbols placed in the context at the end of the material used. No space is left between the last letter of the word and the raised number or symbol. Numbering may be consecutive on each page, consecutive throughout a chapter, or consecutive throughout the text. Footnotes may be in block form or in indented form. Numbers at the beginning of footnotes may be raised a half space above the line of writing or written on the line.

The sequential order of information in footnotes and various methods of handling information in footnotes are illustrated in the following examples:

(A) Book with one author:

1. Raymond V. Lesikar, Business Communication, Theory and Application, Revised Edition, p. 64.

(B) Book with two authors:

2. Billy J. Hodge and Herbert J. Johnson, Management and Organizational Behavior, p. 15.

(C) Book with three authors:

3. Michael T. Matteson, Roger N. Blakeney, and Donald R. Domm, Contemporary Personnel Management, p. 29.

(D) Book with more than three authors:

4. William J. Wasmuth, et al., Human Resources Administration: Problems of Growth and Change, p. 195.

(E) Edited book:

5. Delbert McGuire, ed., Proceedings of the 14th Annual (1971) Institute in Technical and Industrial Communication, p. iv.

(F) Book by one author, revised by another:

6. James A. Gentry, Jr., and Glenn L. Johnson, Finney and Miller's Principles of Accounting, Advanced, Sixth Edition, p. 99.

or

    6. Finney and Miller, <u>Finney and Miller's Principles of</u> <u>Accounting, Advanced</u>, Sixth Edition, revised by James A. Gentry, Jr., and Glenn L. Johnson, p. 99.

(G) Article in an anthology: (Use original source when possible.)

    7. Peter M. Blau, "A Formal Theory of Differentiation in Organizations," printed in W. E. Scott and L. L. Cummings, <u>Readings in Organizational Behavior and Human Performance</u>, Revised Edition, pp. 256-270, article reprinted from <u>American</u> <u>Sociological Review</u>, Vol. 35, No. 2, April, 1970, pp. 201-218.

(H) Book of the Bible:

    8. John 3:16. (Note: Books of the Bible are not underscored.)

(I) Magazine article:

    9. William Schupp, "Any Company Can," <u>Personnel Journal</u>, July, 1973, pp. 629-632.

(J) Association authorship:

    10. Association of MBA Executives, <u>Summitt's 1973 Employ-</u><u>ment Guide</u>, p. 23.

(K) Committee authorship:

    11. Business Liaison Committee, "Around the Business Schools," <u>The Business Graduate</u>, Business Graduates Association Limited, March, 1973, p. 16.

(L) Unpublished speech:

    12. Richard G. Burger, "Putting Resource Management to Work," a speech at the national meeting of the American Institute for Decision Sciences, New Orleans, Louisiana, July 1, 1973.

(M) Published speech:

    13. Charles R. Klasson, "Implementation of PPBS: A Strategy for Professional Accommodation and Organizational Development," address at the Western Association of Collegiate Schools of Business Conference, October 21, 1971, Tucson, Arizona, printed in <u>American Association of Collegiate Schools</u> <u>of Business Bulletin</u>, Vol. 8, No. 2, January, 1972, p. 11.

(N) Quotation in a newspaper:

    14. John McKegney, quoted in <u>The Wall Street Journal</u>, August 10, 1973, p. 1, col. 4.

(O) Personal interview:

    15. Maurice King, Manager, Smith Department Store, Fayetteville, Arkansas, Personal interview with Albert Black, July 31, 1973.

(P) Personal letter:

   16.　John A. Brown, Personal letter to Robert Q. Jones, January 13, 1974.

(Q) Secondhand material: (Use original source if possible.)

   17.　W. Stanley Jevons, The Theory of Political Economy, 4th ed., London, 1911, p.165, (Originally published in 1871) referred to by Jacob Oser, The Evolution of Economic Thought, p. 173.

(R) Unpublished thesis or dissertation:

   18.　Betty Jean Brown, The Relationship Between Supervisor and Student Evaluations of Teaching Effectiveness of General Business Teachers, Unpublished doctoral dissertation, The University of Tennessee at Knoxville, 1971, p. 87.

(S) Author unknown:

   19.　The Wall Street Journal, Staff Reporter, "American Electric Sets Coal-Transfer Facility," August 13, 1973, p. 2, col. 1.

   20.　"Coal Output Rose in Week," The Wall Street Journal, August 10, 1973, p. 2, col. 3.

(T) Government documents:

   21.　United States Department of Labor, Manpower Report of the President, A Report on Manpower Requirements, Resources, Utilization, and Training, Transmitted to the Congress, March, 1973, p. 8.

(U) Encyclopedia article:

   22.　"Economic Productivity," Encyclopedia Britannica, Vol. VII, pp. 930-936.

(V) Law cases:

   23.　Globe Refining Co. v. Landa Cotton Oil Co., 190 U.S. 540, 23 Sup. Ct. 754.

In footnote 23, "190 U.S. 540" means Volume 190, page 540, in the U.S. Government publication, United States Supreme Court Reports; "23 Sup. Ct. 754" means Volume 23, page 754, of the Supreme Court Reporter, published by the West Publishing Company.

   24.　Piekarsky v. Rossman, 95 F. Supp. 748.

In footnote 24, "95 F. Supp. 748" means Volume 95, page 748, of the Federal Supplement, a U.S. Government publication in which U.S. District Court cases appear.

State supreme court cases are handled in the same style as U.S. Supreme Court cases except the name of the state is used instead of "U.S."

Footnotes may be shortened somewhat by using Latin terms or abbreviations for Latin terms.

Examples:

1. Billy J. Hodge and Herbert J. Johnson, Management and Organizational Behavior, passim, pp. 25-36.
2. Ibid.
3. Raymond V. Lesikar, Business Communication, Theory and Application, Revised Edition, p. 64.
4. Ibid., p. 83.
5. _____ , Report Writing for Business, Third Edition, p. 96.
6. Hodge and Johnson, op. cit., p. 93.
7. Lesikar, Report Writing for Business, loc. cit.

Passim means here and there.

Ibid. means the reference just cited. Different pages may be cited as in the fourth footnote.

The blank space in the fifth footnote simply eliminates the typing of the immediately preceding name.

In the sixth footnote, *op. cit.* means in the work cited but not the one immediately preceding.

In the seventh footnote *loc. cit.* means in the exact passage cited.

Footnotes may be placed in at least three positions: (1) at the bottom of the page on which they are mentioned in the text, (2) at the ends of chapters, or (3) within the text.

When placed at the bottom of a page, single-space after the last typewritten line of the text, type a 1½-inch line beginning at the left margin; double-space after the line before starting to type the footnote. Footnotes are single spaced with double spacing between footnotes, and the first line of each footnote is usually indented. The bottom line of the last footnote should be one inch from the bottom edge of the paper. If a footnote is used on a partial page of text, the footnote should be placed at the bottom of the page in its usual location with blank space left between the text and the line placed before the footnote. All of a footnote must be placed on one page. It should not be carried over to the succeeding page.

Example:

Chapter II is a description of the tools of research used in making

_____

1. Raymond V. Lesikar, Business Communication, Theory and Application, Revised Edition, p. 64.

When footnotes are placed at the ends of chapters, they are typed in the same style as when they are typed at the bottoms of the pages. They are headed *Footnotes.*

When typed in the text, they may be handled in two ways. First, they are typed in the same style as when typed at the bottom of the page but are separated from the text by underscores and are double spaced.

Example:

if not the most important quality, a businessman can possess.[1]

_____

    1. Raymond V. Lesikar, Business Communication, Theory and Application, Revised Edition, p. 64.

_____

In the developmental stages of the American economy, written

The second method of handling footnotes in the text is to present in parentheses a shortened, numerical reference to the bibliography and the page number.

Example:

if not the most important quality, a businessman can possess. (14:126)

The first number, "14", is the number of the book, document, or serial in the bibliography. The second number, "126," is the number of the page from which the reference is taken. The colon merely separates the two numbers.

The following abbreviations are often used in footnotes:

anon	anonymous
art. (arts.)	article (articles)
bk. (bks.)	book (books)
ca. (circa)	about
cf.	compare
ch. (chs.)	chapter (chapters)
chap.	chapter
col. (cols.)	column (columns)
ed. (eds.)	editor (editors), edition, edited by
e. g.	for example
et. al.	and others
et seq.	and the following
f. (ff.)	and following page, line, or verse (pages, lines, or verses)
fig. (figs.)	figure (figures)

i.e.	that is
Ibid.	in the same place
Idem or Id.	Idem (the author just cited but not in the book just cited)
illus.	illustrated
infra.	below
l. (ll.)	line (lines)
loc. cit.	in the place cited,
MS (MSS)	manuscript (manuscripts)
no. (nos.)	number (numbers)
op. cit.	in the work cited
p. (pp.)	page (pages)
passim	here and there
rev.	revised, revision
sec. (secs.)	section (sections)
ser.	series
sic.	thus, exactly as quoted (confirms a word that might be questioned)
supra	above or see above
trans.	translated, translator, or translation
v. (vv.)	verse (verses)
viz.	namely
vol. (vols.)	volume (volumes)
v., vs.	versus

(Note: Latin words and their abbreviations are underscored.)

Bibliography

Bibliographies are placed at the ends of reports and are single spaced with double spacing between items. The items may be numbered consecutively throughout the bibliography. Lengthy bibliographies should be classified by types of material. The bibliography usually is separated from the body of the report by a sheet of paper with only "Bibliography" in upper-case letters centered on it. On the first page "Bibliography" is typed two inches from the top of the page. The first entry or the first classification is placed a triple space below the title.

Bibliographies may be punctuated in several ways, but here are two acceptable styles:

Examples: Weeks, Francis W., Principles of Business Communication, Stipes Publishing Company, Champaign, Illinois, 1973.

Weeks, Francis W. Principles of Business Communication. Champaign, Illinois: Stipes Publishing Company, 1973.

Items in a bibliography are placed in alphebetical order by authors' surnames within their respective types of publications. The following sample bibliography shows how the bibliography would be constructed for the references mentioned in the footnote examples on pages 27-31.

BIBLIOGRAPHY

Books

1. Blau, Peter M., "A Formal Theory of Differentiation in Organizations," printed in W. E. Scott and L. L. Cummings, Readings in Organizational Behavior and Human Performance, Revised Edition, Richard D. Irwin, Inc., Homewood, Illinois 60430, 1973, article reprinted from American Sociological Review, Vol. 35, No. 2, April, 1970, pp. 201-218.

    (Note: If the original source of this item were the primary citation, it would be alphabetized under Serials.)

2. Gentry, Jr., James A., and Glenn L. Johnson, Finney and Miller's Principles of Accounting, Advanced, Sixth Edition, Prentice-Hall, Inc., Englewood Cliffs, New Jersey, 1971.

    or

2. Finney and Miller, Finney and Miller's Principles of Accounting, Advanced, revised by James A. Gentry, Jr., and Glenn L. Johnson, Prentice-Hall, Inc., Englewood Cliffs, New Jersey, 1971.

3. Hodge, Billy J., and Herbert J. Johnson, Management and Organizational Behavior, John Wiley & Sons Inc., New York, 1970.

4. Jevons, W. Stanley, The Theory of Political Economy, 4th ed., Macmillan, London, 1911 (Originally published in 1871) referred to by Jacob Oser, The Evolution of Economic Thought, Harcourt, Brace & World, Inc., New York, 1963.

5. John 3:16.

6. Lesikar, Raymond V., Business Communication, Theory and Application, Revised Edition, Richard D. Irwin, Inc., Homewood, Illinois 60430, 1972.

7. _____ , Report Writing for Business, Third Edition, Richard D. Irwin, Inc., Homewood, Illinois 60430, 1969.

8. Matteson, Michael T., Roger N. Blakeney, and Donald R. Domm, Contemporary Personnel Management, Canfield Press, San Francisco, 1972.

9. McGuire, Delbert, ed., Proceedings of the 14th Annual (1971) Institute in Technical and Industrial Communication, Colorado State University, Fort Collins, Colorado, 1971.

10. Wasmuth, William J., et al., Human Resources Administration: Problems of Growth and Change, Houghton Mifflin Company, Boston, 1970.

11. Weeks, Francis W., Principles of Business Communication, Stipes Publishing Company, Champaign, Illinois, 1973.

Encyclopedia

12. Encyclopedia Britannica, Vol. VII, "Economic Productivity," Encyclopedia Britannica, Inc., Chicago, 1969.

Government Documents

13. United States Department of Labor, Manpower Report of the President, A Report on Manpower Requirements, Resources, Utilization, and Training, Transmitted to the Congress, March, 1973, U.S. Government Printing Office, Washington, D.C. 20402, 1973.

Manuscripts

14. Brown, Betty Jean, The Relationship Between Supervisor and Student Evaluations of Teaching Effectiveness of General Business Teachers, Unpublished doctoral dissertation, The University of Tennessee at Knoxville, 1971.

Law Cases

15. Globe Refining Co. v. Landa Cotton Oil Co., 190 U.S. 540, 23 Sup. Ct. 754.

16. Piekarsky v. Rossman, 95 F. Supp. 748.

Letters and Interviews

17. Brown, John A., Personal Letter to Robert Q. Jones, January 13, 1974.

18. King, Maurice Manager, Smith Department Store, Fayetteville, Arkansas, Personal interview with Albert Black, July 31, 1973.

Pamphlets

19. Association of MBA Executives, Summitt's 1973 Employment Guide, Summit Publishing Company, Inc., New York, 1972.

Serials

20. Business Liaison Committee, "Around the Business Schools," Business Graduates Association Limited, The Business Graduate, Vol. 11, No. 4, London, March, 1973.

21. Klasson, Charles R., "Implementation of PPBS: A Strategy for Professional Accommodation and Organizational Development," address at the Western Association of Collegiate Schools of Business Conference, October 21, 1971, Tucson, Arizona, printed in American Association of Collegiate Schools of Business Bulletin, Vol. 8, No. 2, January, 1972, p. 11.

22. McKegney, John, quoted in The Wall Street Journal, August 10, 1973, p. 1, col. 4.

23. Schupp, William, "Any Company Can," Personnel Journal, July, 1973, Vol. 72, No. 7, pp. 629-632.

24. The Wall Street Journal, Staff Reporter, "American Electric Sets Coal-Transfer Facility," August 13, 1973, p. 2, col. 1.

25. _____, "Coal Output Rose in Week," August 10, 1973, p. 2, col. 3.

Speeches

26. Burger, Richard G., "Putting Resource Management to Work," a speech before the national meeting of the American Institute for Decision Sciences, New Orleans, Louisiana, July 1, 1973.

TABLE CONSTRUCTION

Tables may be useful devices for presenting large amounts of information in minimum space. However, to serve their purposes, tables must be designed to present data in logical and orderly fashion, revealing information with proper perspective and appropriate emphasis.

Tables supplement and support context but generally do not replace it. Context is not to be constructed around tables; tables are to be constructed to fit into context because the context guides the reader and points out the specific data the reader should note. Furthermore, without direction provided by context, a reader may not seek information from a table on his own initiative.

Tables may be placed in the context of the body of a report, or they may be placed in an appendix. If the reader's attention is called to specific data in a table, the table should be placed in the body on the page immediately following the reference to the table if the table is typed on a separate page. If a table is placed on a page containing context, the table should be typed, if possible, immediately following the line of writing in which the table is referred to. If not enough room is available to type the entire table in this place, fill the page with context and put the table on the following page. If the table is on the same page as the reference to it, only the table number is mentioned in the text; however, if the table is placed on another page, both the table number and the page number should be mentioned in the text. When casual reference is made to the general content of supplementary material appearing in a table, the table may be placed in an appendix.

The margins of tables should not be smaller than the margins of the textual material. Wide tables may be typed running horizontally on the 11-inch length of the page with the top of the table at the left binding.

Sample Tables 1, 2, and 3 are presented on pages 38, 40, 42, and 43 to show the handling of various problems of tabular presentation.

Parts of a table

Every table has six essential parts: (1) the table number; (2) the title of the table; (3) the stub; (4) the captions; (5) the body; and (6) the source of the table.

4

TABLE 1

SALARIES AND WAGES PAID ALL EMPLOYEES
BY MANUFACTURING IN THE UNITED STATES
(In millions of dollars)
1961-1970

Year	Salaries and Wages Paid	Year	Salaries and Wages Paid
1961	$ 91,646,442[a]	1966	$116,126,224[f]
1962	99,992,091[b]	1967	121,059,493[g]
1963	105,140,558[c]	1968	123,354,003[h]
1964	112,590,424[d]	1969	117,749,749[i]
1965	109,976,667[e]	1970	129,646,442[j]

Sources:

[a] United States Department of Commerce, Bureau of the Census, Annual Survey of Manufactures: 1960 and 1961, Washington, 1963, p. 17.

[b] _____, Annual Survey of Manufactures: 1962, Washington, 1964, p. 14.

[c] _____, Annual Survey of Manufactures: 1965, Washington, 1967, p. 25.

[d] Ibid., p. 24.

[e] _____, Annual Survey of Manufactures: 1966, Washington, 1968, p. 13.

[f] Ibid, p. 12.

[g] _____, Annual Survey of Manufactures: 1967, Washington, 1969, p. 16

[h] _____, Annual Survey of Manufactures: 1968, Washington, 1970, p. 8.

[i] _____, Census of Manufactures: 1970, Volume II, Industry Statistics, Washington, 1972, pp. 1-6.

[j] _____, Annual Survey of Manufactures: 1970 and 1971, Washington, 1973, p. 29.

(Sample Vertical Table)

Numbering of tables. Tables may be numbered in Arabic or Roman numerals in either of two ways: (1) consecutively throughout the body of the report or (2) consecutively throughout each chapter. When numbered by chapter, the number of the chapter is given and is followed by a period and the number of the table:

Examples:　Table 1.1 (i.e., Chapter 1, Table 1)
　　　　　　Table 1.2 (i.e., Chapter 1, Table 2)
　　　　　　Table 2.1 (i.e., Chapter 2, Table 1)
　　　　　　Table 2.2 (i.e., Chapter 2, Table 2)

This style is used only in lengthy reports containing many tables.

Titles of tables. The title of a table should contain the following information: (1) the description of the data — tell what the data are; (2) the reference of the data — tell to what the data refer, e.g., the geographical location or the name of the company; (3) the classification of the data; and (4) the time period covered if appropriate. Titles of tables are usually typed in upper-case letters and are centered a single space above the table, and each line after the first line should ideally be shorter than the preceding one. Don't break phrases.

Occasionally the table number and the title of a table are combined as follows:

TABLE 1. – Simple Index Numbers for Manufacturing
　　　　　　Employment, United States, West North Central
　　　　　　Region, and Oklahoma, 1949-1969. (1957=100)

Only the important words are capitalized in this style. Whatever the style selected, that style should be used on all tables throughout the report.

Captions. Captions are columnar headings, which describe the data in the columns of the table. Capitalize all important words in captions. Subcaptions are used to show subdivisions of main captions. Captions and subcaptions, which must be concise and clear, are centered over their respective columns. Occasionally captions are typed perpendicular to the columns they describe. When typed in this fashion, they should be typed so that the page may be turned clockwise one-quarter turn for reading. (See Table 1, p. 38.)

Stub. The stub of a table is the left column, which contains descriptions of the data extended across the table to the right. Stub descriptions must have parallel structure and be indented two or three spaces under the preceding line. (See "Report Mechanics," p. 25, for a discussion of parallel structure in headings.) The first word of each item is capitalized. If an item requires more than one line, succeeding lines should be indented two or three spaces. Leaders may be used after each description to guide the reader to the columns.

TABLE 2

RESULTS OF COOPERATIVE ENGLISH TEST GIVEN TO STUDENTS IN THREE TYPES OF COLLEGES

Total Scores

Classes of Students	Types of Colleges								
	Type I Preprofessional			Type II Liberal Arts			Type III Junior-Teacher College		
	Number	Mean	Standard Deviation	Number	Mean	Standard Deviation	Number	Mean	Standard Deviation
Entering Freshmen	1,800	60.3	9.2	9,000	55.6	9.3	2,200	58.1	9.4
Freshmen	1,400	62.4	9.2	7,500	57.4	9.3	2,000	51.3	9.4
Sophomores	5,500	64.0	9.3	27,000	59.3	9.4	8,000	54.2	9.5
Juniors	700	65.2	9.4	4,000	60.5	9.5	1,200	65.3	9.5
Seniors	600	66.2	9.4	2,500	61.6	9.5	600	58.5	9.6
Totals . .	10,000			50,000			14,000		

Source: Cooperative Test Division, Educational Testing Service, Princeton, New Jersey

(Sample Horizontal Table)

Body. The body of the table contains the actual tabulated data and should be placed in logical and orderly fashion. Items may be either single or double spaced. All numbers in each column are aligned on the right. Decimal points should be aligned vertically. Unit symbols are typed by the first number in the column and by the numbers following total and subtotal rulings. The dollar sign is placed one space to the left of the longest line in the column and is typed on the line with the first number. Dated data should be arranged with the oldest data in the left column and the most recent data in the right column. Commas should be used to separate millions from thousands and thousands from hundreds.

Totals are usually placed at the bottom of the data with *total* indented, but for some data the total may be given at the top of the columns. (See Table 3, pp. 42 and 43.) To aid readability in a large single-spaced table, items may be arranged in groups of five items with double spaces between the groups. Data not available are indicated by three hyphens, three periods, or *n.a.* for "not available."

Source. The source from which the tabulated data were obtained must be shown at the bottom of a table. Multiple sources are indicated by lower-case, superior letters. (See Table 1, p. 38.) Only if the data are original may the source not be shown.

Footnotes

Footnotes for tables are indicated by raised, lower-case letters, asterisks, daggers, or other symbols. The footnotes are typed below the horizontal line following tabulated data and precede the source notation. (See Table 3, p. 43.) Footnotes may be indented or blocked at the left margin. Always double-space between the footnotes. Also, double-space between sources and between the footnotes and the source.

Tabular rulings

A double-line, horizontal ruling is placed a single space below the title of a table. This placement is the same as a double space above the top line of the table captions.

A single-line, horizontal ruling is placed between a main caption and a subcaption. This ruling is typed on the same line as the main caption, and the subcaption is typed on the next line below.

A single-line, horizontal ruling is placed a single space below the last line of subcaptions or a double space above the first line of the body of a table.

A double-line, horizontal ruling is placed a single space below the body of a table, i.e., a double space above the first footnote or source notation.

Vertical rulings are seldom used in typewritten tables; however, they may be used to separate columns if needed for readability. Vertical rulings may extend the full length of a table or may extend

8

TABLE 3

KANSAS EMPLOYMENT BY ECONOMIC SECTOR
1950-1971

Economic Sector	1950		1955		1960		1965	
	Employees	Per-cent	Employees	Per-cent	Employees	Per-cent	Employees	Per-cent
Total employment	724,000	100*	781,500	100	769,700	100	789,700	100
Agriculture	171,300	24	143,000	18	112,200	14	96,000	12
Manufacturing	95,300	13	128,900	16	116,000	15	122,200	15
Durable	42,500	6	76,000	10	65,300	8	72,300	9
Nondurable	52,800	7	52,900	6	50,700	6	49,900	6
Mining	17,200	2	19,300	2	17,000	2	13,700	2
Contract construction	30,000	4	37,500	5	33,900	4	33,200	4
Transportation, communication, electric, gas, and sanitation service	63,500	9	64,800	8	53,700	7	50,400	6
Wholesale and retail trade	109,700	15	118,900	15	130,200	17	138,400	18
Finance, insurance, and real estate	16,300	2	19,800	3	23,300	3	26,000	3
Services	51,300	7	58,800	8	69,900	9	83,800	11
Government	80,500	11	95,800	12	115,000	15	132,500	17
All other	88,900	12	94,700	12	98,500	13	93,500	12

(Sample Continuing Table)

9

TABLE 3 (Continued)

Economic Sector	1968		1969		1970		1971	
	Employees	Per-Cent	Employees	Per-Cent	Employees	Per-Cent	Employees	Per-Cent
Total employment	839,700	100	849,900	100	837,600	100	842,100	100
Agriculture	82,100	10	77,900	9	75,100	9	80,200	10
Manufacturing	147,900	18	147,600	17	134,500	16	129,800	15
Durable	92,400	11	91,600	11	78,500	9	73,600	9
Nondurable	55,500	7	56,000	6	56,000	7	56,200	6
Mining	11,700	1	11,600	1	11,000	1	10,000	1
Contract construction	34,000	4	34,100	4	32,000	4	31,200	4
Transportation, communication, electric, gas, and sanitation service	51,700	6	52,100	6	52,300	6	51,200	6
Wholesale and retail trade	152,800	18	157,800	19	159,300	19	162,100	19
Finance, insurance, and real estate	28,500	3	29,700	3	30,400	4	30,900	4
Services	97,200	12	100,600	12	103,000	12	104,500	12
Government	147,100	17	150,800	18	154,500	18	156,300	19
All other	87,900	11	87,700	10	85,500	10	85,900	10

*Percentages were calculated by the author of this report.

Source: Kansas Statistical Abstract 1972, The Institute for Social and Environmental Studies, The University of Kansas, Lawrence, Kansas, 1973, p. 99.

(Sample Continuing Table)

only through the captions. (See Table 2, p. 40.) Rulings may be typed or drawn with india ink.

To avoid the awkward appearance of a long table with only two or three captions, the data may be presented in two identical columns separated by a vertical line.

Multiple-page tables

Tables that can be placed on one page should not be divided and typed on two pages. Occasionally data may require more columns than can be put on one page, or a table may be too long for a page. In either case the table has to be enlarged.

Tables may be enlarged in either of two ways. First, enough additional paper may be cemented to the regular 8½-by-11-inch stationery to accommodate a large table. The typed table would be inserted into the report and folded in accordion style. Enlarged pages with accordion folds should be used for the addition of only two or three columns or for tables requiring frequent comparisons of columnar data.

Second, for tables not requiring frequent comparison of columnar data or for tables that would make unwieldy foldouts, simply construct additional tables, using captions and stub descriptions identical to those on the first page. (See Table 3, pp. 42 and 43.) The title of the table need not be repeated on continued pages; but the table number should be given, e.g., Table 1 (Continued).

Footnotes, sources, and double-line rulings following the body are given only on the last page of a table.

Pagination

Every page of a table must have a page number placed in the same position as on other pages in the text. At times, when pages have large tables, page numbers may be moved slightly toward the margins.

Proofreading is a skill developed by concentrated practice, not one automatically possessed simply because you can read.

To become a good proofreader, you must want to see errors in writing; you must want to present error-free copy. Without such desires, an attempt at proofreading is simply wasted time.

Proofreading skill

Although proofreading skill may be developed in several ways, here is a technique that may be used to develop proofreading ability:

1. Read the copy rapidly to see whether the context makes sense.
2. Read the copy again but very slowly the second time. Forget about content and concentrate on mechanics. Question the spelling of every word, the placement of every punctuation mark, and the order of words and figures. Check the capitalization of proper nouns and the spelling of every word about which you have the slightest doubt.

In the second reading, reread questionable phrases and sentences and search for hidden meanings. Even the most innocent statement may be interpreted strangely by a reader.

Here are some examples of well-intended statements that may very well distract the reader:

1. "The Mets had three on base." (Knowing the history of the Mets, a well-informed person may logically ask, "Which base?")
2. "Safety ashtrays will put an end to burn-marked furniture." (The ashtrays will destroy the furniture?)
3. "Buy several ashtrays—enough to cover every room adequately!"
4. "The fire fighters extinguished the house."
5. "A total of 80,000 employees fell to 63,000."
6. "Please request the doctor to return her form to our office in the enclosed envelope."

Proofreading errors

Following are types of errors that are frequently overlooked when proofreading:

1. Abbreviations incorrect
2. Addresses incorrect or incomplete

3. Alignment of columns incorrect
4. Antecedent omitted or not clear
5. Apostrophe incorrectly placed

   Example: It's for possessive pronoun its

6. Apostrophe omitted

   Example: We are having a sale of mens suits.

7. Capitalization errors
8. Line continued from one page to another
9. Decimal point omitted
10. Divisions of words at ends of lines incorrect
11. Enclosure notation at the end of a letter omitted
12. Figures incorrect
13. Grammatical errors

    Example: This amount will be paid to you in a lump
             sum at the time of your death, which
             we believe is what you desire. (The
             money cannot be paid to a dead person,
             and *which* has an incorrect antecedent.

14. Confusion of homonyms, such as *their-there, hear-here, fair-fare, ware-wear.*

    Example: Our supervisor is very much interested in the
             control of waste (not *waist*).

15. Hyphenated nouns and adjectives
16. Letter omitted or added

    Example: occassion for occasion or accomodate for
             accommodate

17. Letters transposed, especially *i* and *e.*

    Examples: How old is your two-headed (for *tow-
              headed*) son?
              Untied States for United States
              casual for causal or causal for casual

18. Mailing notations omitted from letters
19. Modifiers out of place
20. Page numbers omitted or incorrect
21. Paragraphing inappropriate
22. Paragraphs not indented
23. Punctuation faulty
24. Quotation marks, especially closing a quotation, omitted
25. Repetition of words

26. Sentences incomplete
27. Spacing between words or within words
28. Spelling of names, such as *Kelly-Kelley, Stephens-Stevens, Wolf-Wolfe, Pearson-Pierson, Lang-Laing, Anderson-Andersen, Brown-Browne.*
29. Underscore omitted
30. Words misspelled

    Example: Santa <u>Clause</u> instead of Santa <u>Claus</u>

31. Words transposed

Proofreaders' marks

Here are some commonly accepted marks used in proofreading to indicate errors, corrections, and changes on rough-draft copy:

stet	let it stand
⌒ or *tr.*	transpose
ctr.	center
#	insert space
sp.	spell out or spell correctly
¶	paragraph
No ¶	no paragraph
⌐	move to right
⌐	move to left
⌣	move down
⌢	move up
sc	use small capitals
ital	use italics
⌣⌣⌣	use boldface
bf.	boldface
lc.	lower case (change capital to small letter)
caps	use capitals
=	capitalize (Place lines under letter to be capitalized.)
⌒	close space
∨	insert superior letter, figure, or material in margin
∧	insert inferior letter, figure, or material in margin
//	straighten margin
ℓ	delete
⌐	start new line

GRAMMAR PROBLEMS V

Perhaps the poorest method of determining correct grammar usage is by the way something sounds. "If it sounds correct, it is correct" simply will not work unless what is used to being heard is correct. What is used to being heard is what will sound correct but may be incorrect.

A complete review of grammar is far beyond the scope of this style manual; however, several points of grammar that frequently cause trouble are presented.

Agreement of subjects and verbs

1. *A lot* as a subject takes a plural verb when *of* is followed by a plural noun.

> Examples: A lot of books were borrowed.
> A lot of mail was delivered to wrong addresses.

2. When *some*, *all*, or *any* refers to several things, the verb is plural.

> Examples: All of the envelopes were soiled.
> All of the grain was weighed.
> Some of the men attend meetings regularly.
> Any of the secretaries are welcome to attend.

3. None is usually considered to be singular because it means *no one;* however, *none* frequently may take a plural verb if it is followed by a plural noun or pronoun. If the idea of *no one* is emphasized, a singular verb is used.

> Examples: None of the workers was hurt.
> None of them are going with us.
> None was enthusiastic about the project.

4. Phrases placed between a subject and a verb do not affect the number of the verb, which must agree with the subject.

> Examples: The result of his findings was published.
> She, together with her sisters, was initiated.
> The instructions of the supervisor were followed carefully.

5. When a fraction is used as a subject and followed by *of* and a plural noun, the verb is plural; when the fraction is followed by *of* and a singular noun, the verb is singular.

Examples: Two thirds of the report is completed.
Two thirds of the reports are completed.

6. *Here* and *there* may introduce sentences, but the verb agrees with the subject following the verb.

Examples: Here is an example of good writing.
Here are examples of good writing.
There is the report.
There are the reports.

7. *Both . . . and,* used in a compound subject, requires a plural verb.

Example: Both Mr. Fields and his secretary are attending the meeting.

8. Relative pronouns may be singular or plural, depending on whether the antecedent is singular or plural.

Examples: She is one of the members who were absent.
(Antecedent is *members.*)
She was the only member who was absent.
(Antecedent is *member*).

9. Compound subjects require plural verbs unless the subjects are preceded by *every, each,* or *many a.*

Examples: John and his employer are on their vacations.
Every member and his employer was present.
Each manager and his assistant was at the meeting.
Many a man and his sons has made that sacrifice.

10. When *either . . . or* and *neither . . . nor* have singular nouns or pronouns as second subjects, the verbs are singular. When the second subject is a plural noun or pronoun, the verb is plural.

Examples: Either Mr. Finch or his assistant is coming.
Either Mr. Finch or his assistants are coming.
Neither you nor I am responsible for the damage.
Neither he nor they are responsible for the disturbance.

11. In contrasted expressions the verb should agree with the positive expression.

Example: The department head, not his assistants, is to be rewarded.

12. *Each, each one, either, everyone, someone, somebody, anybody, anyone, nobody, no one,* and *neither,* used as subjects, take singular verbs.

> Examples: Each has done excellent work.
> Neither has made an error.
> Is either of you going?

13. A compound subject consisting of singular nouns joined by *and* requires a plural verb.

> Examples: The secretary and the treasurer (two people) are late.
> The secretary and treasurer (one person holding two jobs) is late.
> The secretary-treasurer (one person) is late.

14. Singular subjects joined by *or* or *nor* require singular verbs.

> Examples: The secretary or the treasurer is absent.
> Neither the secretary nor the treasurer is absent.

15. *Number* preceded by *the* must be followed by a singular verb. *Number* preceded by *a* must be followed by a plural verb.

> Examples: The number of employees absent is small.
> A number of houses were damaged by the high winds.

Anticipatory subjects

Although beginning sentences and independent clauses with *it* and *there* is not incorrect, avoid starting sentences and clauses with these words. These beginnings are called anticipatory subjects because they come before the true subjects of the sentences or clauses. Anticipatory subjects cause wordiness and delay the central ideas of sentences.

> Examples: Being punctual is important. (or) Punctuality is important. (Not: It is important to be punctual.)
> Today is beautiful. (Not: It is a beautiful day.)
> We based our action on these premises. (Not: It is upon these premises that we based our action.)
> Many people attended the convention. (Not: There were many people attending the convention.)
> Seven members will be on the committee. (Not: There will be seven members on the committee.)

Collective nouns

1. Collective nouns specify groups of people or things. Some common collective nouns are:

abundance	crowd	pair
all	enemy	people
any	faculty	plenty
assembly	family	police
audience	firm	proportion (fractional parts)
band	group	rest
board	jury	some
bulk	majority	United States
class	minority	variety
club	more	youth
commission	most	
committee	multitude	
company	none	
corporation	number	
couple	orchestra	

2. Depending upon the intended meaning, collective nouns may take either singular or plural verbs. A plural verb is used when the individual parts of the collective unit are considered separately. A singular verb is used when the parts are considered as a single unit.

> Examples: The faculty supports academic freedom. (The faculty as a unit)
> The faculty are debating academic freedom. (The individual members are debating among themselves.)
> All are going. (All members are going.)
> All is too much. (The total is too much.)
> The youth are vigorous. (The youngsters are vigorous.)
> The youth is an important segment of the population.
> Half are sold. (Two of four are sold.)
> Half is to be distributed. (A portion is to be distributed.)
> In the battle 375 enemy were killed.

3. Collective nouns are frequently used with plural verbs when prepositional phrases appear between the nouns and the verbs.

> Examples: A majority of the members were present.
> A number of items were damaged.
> The youth of America is (or are) vigorous.

4. To avoid expressions that may sound awkward, collective nouns are often used as adjectives or are placed in prepositional phrases.

Examples: The board members are present. (The board are
                present.)
             The members of the family are going. (The family
                are going.)
             Some members are going. (Some are going.)
             Half of the items are sold. (Half are sold.)

5. Collective nouns cause little trouble for writers because what
   sounds correct is usually correct. However, considerable trouble
   arises from the use of pronouns that refer to collective nouns.
   When a collective noun is treated as a plural noun, its pronoun
   must be plural. Conversely, when a collective noun is treated as
   a singular noun, its pronoun must be singular.

Examples: Collectives:
             The family are taking their (not *its*) vacation this
                week.
             The board agree to give their (not *its*) decision
                tomorrow.
             The majority are registering their (not *its*) votes.

             Singulars:
             The family is taking its (not *their*) vacation this
                week.
             The board agrees to give its (not *their*) decision
                tomorrow.
             The majority is registering its (not *their*) vote.

6. Closely related to collective nouns are some words that are
   either singular or plural:

acoustics	eaves	measles
aeronautics	economics	mechanics
aesthetics	electronics	moose
amends	elk	mumps
apparatus	ethics	odds
athletics	forceps	offspring
bellows	gross	paraphernalia
chassis	grouse	physics
Chinese	gymnastics	pincers
civics	headquarters	pliers
corps	hysterics	politics
cosmetics	Japanese	rendezvous
cybernetics	mankind	scissors
deer	mathematics	series
dramatics	means	shambles

shears	suds	vermin
sheep	sweepstakes	whereabouts
Sioux	tactics	works
species	tongs	
statistics	tweezers	

7. Some words are always plural or are usually used in the plural:

alms	heroics	shorts
archives	leavings	spectacles
belongings	nuptials	thanks
brains	pants	trousers
cattle	police	wages

clothes	premises
gentry	proceeds
glasses	remains
goods	riches
gross	series

8. Some words are always singular or are usually used in the singular:

celery	news
game (animals and fowls)	nutmeg
lettuce	rhubarb
lightning	vanilla
livestock	wheat
molasses	wildlife

9. Some words have two plurals:

aircraft	Aircraft were flying	Five aircrafts (types)
bass	The bass were caught	The basses of North America
billion	Several billion were	Billions of people
brick	A ton of brick	Ten bricks
buffalo	We hunted buffalo	Two buffalos in the zoo
cannon	Sounds of cannon	Two cannons in the park
cod	Cod were caught	Cods of the Atlantic Ocean
dozen	Five dozen were	Dozens of people were there
duck	Hunt duck	Two ducks in the pond
fish	Fish are in the pond	Fishes of North America
giraffe	Hunt giraffe	Two giraffes in the zoo
head	Six head of cattle	Man with two heads
heathen	The heathen were banished	Two heathens
hundred	Several hundred were	Hundreds of people
lion	Hunt lion	Two lions in the zoo
million	Several million were	Millions were
pair	The pair are	Three pairs of shoes
personnel	The personnel are	The personnels of five companies

quail	We shot quail	Two quails in the cage
salmon	Salmon are in the river	Salmons of North America
score	Four score and seven	Football scores
shot	Pound of shot (ammunition)	Six shots in the dark
thousand	Several thousand were	Thousands of people
turkey	Hunt turkey	Turkeys in the pen
trout	Fish for trout	Trouts of North America
yoke	Two yoke of oxen	Yokes on the dresses

Comparisons

1. The comparative degree of an adjective is used to compare two items.

   The superlative degree of an adjective is used to compare more than two items.

   > Examples: Mr. Moore is taller than Mr. Harris.
   > Mr. Moore is the tallest man in the office.

2. A comparison of two things or two persons in the same class should use the adjective *other*.

   > Examples: Our line of furniture is better than any other line on the market. (Without *other*, the sentence means that our line is better than any other line, including ours. That doesn't make sense!)
   > I like Dallas better than any other Texas city. (Without *other*, the sentence means I like Dallas better than any other Texas city, including Dallas.)

3. Comparisons should always be clear.

   > Example: He is the tallest student in the school. (To say he he is the tallest student *of any* in the school means that he is taller than himself.)

4. *So . . . as* is used in negative expressions. *As . . . as* is used in affirmative expressions.

   > Examples: She was not so early today as she was yesterday.
   > He arrived as early today as he did yesterday.

5. (a)   Many adjectives do not have comparative forms because they represent extreme positions. Here are a few of them:

aboard	favorite	spotless
absolute	final	square
adequate	flat	supreme
alike	ideal	unanimous
appropriate	identical	unique
asleep	immaculate	universal
circular	impossible	utmost
complete	infinite	worthless
conclusive	level	wrecked
continual	minimal	wrong
correct	odorless	
dead	open	
definite	opposite	
destroy	parallel	
difficult	perfect	
endless	perpendicular	
essential	perpetual	
eternal	right	
extreme	round	
faultless	satisfactory	

(b) Noncomparative adjectives may be modified by such adverbs as *almost*, *nearly*, and *about*.

Examples: The job was almost impossible.
The item is the most nearly perfect one in the group.
The road was about level.

(c) Care should be taken not to use superfluous modifiers with noncomparable adjectives.

Examples: This is correct. (Not: "This is absolutely correct" because, if something is correct, it is absolute.)
The floor was spotless. (Not: completely spotless)
I am going to kill him. (Not: kill him dead)
The twins are identical. (Not: exactly identical)

Compound adjectives

1. Compound adjectives must be written with hyphens when a noun follows:

Examples: That building is a small-animal hospital.
(Without the hyphen, there is no way of knowing whether the animals are small or the hospital is small.

This is up-to-date material.

This material is up to date. (Noun does not follow, therefore, no hyphen.)

Send this package by first-class mail.

This mail is first class.

The building has one-, two-, and three-bedroom apartments.

2. *Well* is the only adverb that may be used as the first word of a compound adjective.

Examples: They prepared well-balanced meals at the cafeteria. This is a well-managed business.

(Note: Adverbs are usually recognized by *ly* endings. Noted exceptions are *leisurely*, *miserly*, *likely*, *friendly*, *slovenly*, and *cowardly*, which are used as either adverbs or adjectives.)

Compound nouns

Compound nouns are tricky. Dictionaries show inconsistencies not only in the compounding of nouns but also in the formations of their plurals. Here are a few compound nouns and their plurals, but a dictionary should be checked for correct spellings when doubt exists.

Singular	*Plural*
brother-in-law	brothers-in-law
charge-a-plate	charge-a-plates
crowfoot	crowfeet (or) crowfoots
crow's-foot	crow's-feet
crow's nest	crow's nests
court-martial	courts-martial (or) court-martials
cupful	cupfuls (or) cupsful
editor in chief	editors in chief
handful	handfuls (or) handsful
handout	handouts
hanger-on	hangers-on
gentleman-commoner	gentlemen-commoners
gentleman friend	gentlemen friends
gentleman-usher	gentlemen-ushers
jack-in-the-box	jack-in-the-boxes (or) jacks-in-the-box
jack-in-the-pulpit	jack-in-the-pulpits (or) jacks-in-the-pulpit
jack-of-all-trades	jacks-of-all-trades
knight bachelor	knights bachelors (or) knights bachelor
Knight Templar	Knights Templars (or) Knights Templar
looker-on	lookers-on
major general	major generals

man-of-war	men-of-war
notary public	notaries public (or) notary publics
passerby	passersby
secretary of state	secretaries of state
son-in-law	sons-in-law
walk-up	walk-ups
walkway	walkways

Dangling participles

Participles must be placed so that they modify appropriate nouns. If the participle does not modify the appropriate noun, the participle dangles; and the meaning is distorted.

Examples: Correct: Looking up the road, we saw a large dog. (We were looking.)

Incorrect: Looking up the road, a big dog was seen. (The dog was looking.)

Correct: Being a retired person, he had a small income. (Not: Being a retired person, his income was small.)

Incorrect: Riding down the street on my bicycle, the dog bit my leg. (Was the dog riding the bicycle?)

Double negatives

Avoid the use of two negatives to express one idea.

Examples: He didn't make any (not *no*) corrections.
He wasn't granted any (not *no*) extra time.
He wasn't anywhere (not *nowhere*) in the store.

Double subjects

Double subjects are unnecessary.

Example: Mr. Jones, after going to the meeting, gave a speech. (Not: Mr. Jones, after going to the meeting, he gave a speech.)

Foreign derivatives

Some words have retained the plural forms used in the languages of their origins:

addendum	addenda
agendum	agenda, agendums
alumna (fm)	alumnae
alumnus (ms)	alumni
analysis	analyses
anamnesis	anamneses
antenna	antennae, antennas
apparatus	apparatus, apparatuses

appendix	appendixes, appendices
automaton	automatons, automata
axis	axes
bacillus	bacilli
bacterium	bacteria
basis	bases
cactus	cacti, cactuses
cherub	cherubs, cherubim
cirrus	cirri
crisis	crises
criterion	criteria, criterions
crocus	crocuses, croci
curriculum	curricula, curriculums
datum	data, datums
diagnosis	diagnoses
die	dice
emphasis	emphases
erratum	errata
focus	focuses, foci
formula	formulas, formulae
fungus	fungi, funguses
gladiolus	gladioli, gladiolus, gladioluses
hypothesis	hypotheses
index	indexes, indices
larva	larvae, larvas
libretto	librettos, libretti
locus	loci
matrix	matrices, matrixes
maximum	maximums, maxima
medium	mediums, media
memorandum	memorandums, memoranda
minutia	minutiae
momentum	momenta, momentums
monsieur	messieurs
moratorium	moratoriums, moratoria
neurosis	neuroses
opus	opera, opuses
ovum	ova
paralysis	paralyses
parenthesis	parentheses
phenomenon	phenomena, phenomenons
plateau	plateaus, plateaux
psychosis	psychoses
radius	radii, radiuses
referendum	referenda, referendums
rostrum	rostrums, rostra

stadium	stadia, stadiums
stimulus	stimuli
stratum	strata
stratus	strati
syllabus	syllabi, syllabuses
synopsis	synopses
synthesis	syntheses
tableau	tableaux, tableaus
thesis	theses
trousseau	trousseaux, trousseaus
vertebra	vertebrae, vertebras
virtuoso	virtuosos, virtuosi

Although many of these words have more than one plural form, the correct plural may be determined by the use of the word.

Examples: 1. Antenna
  (a) The organs of an insect may be either antennae or antennas.
  (b) The devices for radiating and receiving radio waves are usually called antennas.
2. Cherub
  (a) Biblical figures and angels may be either cherubs or cherubim.
  (b) Beautiful children and innocent-looking adults are cherubs.
3. Crocus
  (a) The flowers may be either crocuses or croci.
  (b) The metal polishes are crocuses.
4. Datums is correctly used only when referring to things used as a basis for calculation or measurement.
5. Focus
  (a) Used as a noun, the plural of focus may be either focuses or foci.
  (b) Used as a verb, the singular is focuses.
6. Gladiolus
  (a) The flowers may be called gladioli, gladiolus, or gladioluses.
  (b) The middle portions of sternums are gladioli.
7. Phenomenons is used only to refer to abnormal people, things, or occurrences.
8. Stadiums is usually used to refer to open sports arenas.

Infinitives

1. Infinitives should not be split except to avoid awkward construction.

   Examples: He tried to do the job adequately. (Not: He tried to adequately do the job.)

   The listings could bring additional responses sufficient to more nearly justify the rates charged.

2. Two verbs should not be joined by *and* when an infinitive conveys precise meaning.

   Examples: Come and (also) visit us.

   Come to (in order to) visit us.

   Plan and (also) go.

   Plan to (in order to) go.

   He went to the office and (also) signed some papers.

   He went to the office to (in order to) sign some papers.

Modifiers

To achieve clarity, modifiers should be placed close to the words they modify.

   Examples: Select a house that is for sale in the community. (Not: Select a house in the community that is for sale.)

   In Reno we stopped at the first motel, which had 12 vacancies. (Not: We stopped at the first motel in Reno, which had 12 vacancies.)

   Please return the statement marked "paid" to the store. (Not: Please return the statement to the store marked "paid.")

   In those housing areas, which are very small, each dwelling has only two apartments.

   In those housing areas each dwelling has only two apartments, which are very small.

Omissions

After *than* or *as*, part of a clause may be omitted.

   Examples: We can send your order more quickly than they. (After *they*, "can send your order" is understood.)

   We enjoy buying from your company better than them. (After *than*, "buying from" is understood.)

George likes Mary better than I. (Better than I
like Mary!)
George likes Mary better than me. (Better than
he likes me!)

Parallel structure

1. Two similarly related ideas should be expressed by the same
   construction.

   Examples: They went to transact business and to attend the
                opera.
                He answered neither my letter nor my telegram.
                (Not: He neither answered my letter nor my
                telegram. *Neither* must precede the same part
                of speech that *nor* precedes.)
                The letter either was not written or was lost in
                the mail. (Both *either* and *or* are before verbs.)
                Sara's mother is tall, has short hair, and wears
                light colors. (Not: Sara's mother is tall with
                short hair and wears light colors.)
                Mr. Hughes implied that everything would be
                great and that Mr. Stone would be off his
                back. (Note: *That* is necessary before *Mr.
                Stone* if Hughes implied Mr. Stone would
                be off his back. If this is not the implication,
                a comma should follow *great*; and *that*
                should be deleted because the sentence
                then is a compound sentence.)

2. The person, number, subject, voice, tense, or mood should not
   be shifted unless one has a good reason for making a shift.

   Examples: Incorrect: The board of directors met monthly,
                           and many decisions were made. (A
                           shift from active to passive voice)
                Correct: The board of directors met monthly
                           and made many decisions. (Active
                           voice)
                Incorrect: Sharpen your pencil, fill your pen,
                           and then you open your notebook.
                           (A shift from imperative to
                           declarative mood.)
                Correct: Sharpen your pencil, fill your pen,
                           and then open your notebook.
                           (Imperative mood)

Incorrect: If a person follows directions carefully, they will be successful. (A shift of number from singular to plural)

Correct: If a person follows directions carefully, he will be successful. (Singular number)

Correct: I talked with the president, whose name is George. (A shift of tense! However, to say, "whose name was George," sounds as if George changed his name or died.)

Possessives

1. The possessive singular is expressed by adding 's.

Examples: a month's vacation
the man's hat
the secretary's typewriter
ox's yoke
waitress's table (or) waitress' table
stone's throw
John Smith, Jr.'s, address
The desk is Kay's.
company's stock

2. The possessive plural is expressed by s' when the plural ends in s.

Examples: three months' vacation
secretaries' typewriters
waitresses' tables
companies' stocks

3. The possessive plural is expressed by 's when the plural does not end in s.

Examples: men's hats
women's shoes
oxen's yokes

4. Compound words are made possessive by adding 's to the last word.

Examples: father-in-law's occupation (singular possessive)
fathers-in-law's occupations (plural possessive)

5. Joint ownership is shown by making the last word in the series possessive.

Example: Jim and Dick's car needs cleaning. (The boys own the car jointly.)

6. Separate ownership is shown by making each item possessive.

> Example: Mr. Black's and Mr. Dick's desks need cleaning.
> (Each man owns a desk.)

7. To show possession of inanimate objects, an *of* phrase is preferred to an apostrophe.

> Examples: Preferred: The cover of the book is soiled.
> Correct: The book's cover is soiled.
> Preferred: The stock of the company was sold.
> Correct: The company's stock was sold.
> Preferred: The stocks of the companies were sold
> Correct: The companies' stocks were sold.

8. Possessives of proper nouns that end in *s* may be formed by adding an apostrophe or by adding 's.

> Examples: Jones' car (singular possessive)
> Jones's car (singular possessive)
> Joneses' car (the family car — plural possessive)

9. No apostrophes are used with possessive pronouns.

> Examples: Its, yours, his, hers, theirs

10. Use the possessive case of a noun or a pronoun that modifies a gerund, a verb ending in *ing* used as a noun.

> Examples: Do you understand his reacting as he did?
> He did not object to my doing the work today.
> I appreciate your calling me.
> Martin did not tell us about Mary's calling at our home.
> There is some uncertainty about her going to Milwaukee.
> The company's financing of the project was inadequate.

11. To show possession by a noun that is followed by an appositive, use an apostrophe with the appositive.

> Examples: This is Mr. Smith, the manager's, office.
> This is the manager, Mr. Smith's, office.

12. When possessed items are implied, use the possessive form.

> Examples: Send your order to Weaver's. (*Store* is implied.)
> We bought the supplies from Macy's.
> The car is Jack's.

13. Use the official spellings for company and organizational names. Many of them do not use apostrophes.

> Examples: Veterans Administration
> Teachers College
> Joes Tavern

Prepositions

A sentence should not end with a preposition when the resulting structure is awkward.

> Examples: Where did he go (not go to).
> Where is his office (not office at)?
> When did he check in? (*In* is an adverb.)
> Why did you do that? (Not: What did you do that for?)
> He had the check with which he had paid the bill. (Not: that he had paid the bill with.)

Pronouns

1. A pronoun must agree with its antecedent in gender, number, and person.

> Examples: Everyone in the office must hand in his (not *their*) report
> Everybody at the party talked as if he (not *they*) had an enjoyable evening.
> Any of the officers would be glad to do his share of the work.
> Neither Mr. Lane nor Mr. Marks was permitted to carry out his plans.
> Either Mr. Jones or Mr. Miller will sign his name on the document.
> Either is to sign his name to the petition.
> Neither is to sign his name to the petition.

2. Traditionally the masculine form of a pronoun is used when referring to two genders or when the gender is unknown. Use the neuter gender of pronouns when the sexes of animals, fish, and fowls are unknown.

> Examples: Either Miss Smith or Mr. Stevens will sign his name.
> Lee Jones wrecked his car.
> The bird fell out of its nest.
> (Note: Some affirmative-action programs and the women's liberation movement have opposed using the masculine form for a word in the generic sense. Instead, they suggest

coining words such as *chairperson* for
chairman and using *he or she* for *he.*)

3. All pronouns should have antecedents, and the antecedents
should be clear.

   Examples: I was detained by a fire at my home, and it
   wasn't my fault. (What wasn't my fault?)
   Mr. Jacobs told Mr. Smith that he should do
   the job. (Who should do the job?)
   While on vacation, you will be away from your
   work, which will be good for you. (What
   will be good for you?)
   The original copy was discarded after the
   material was typed. This caused a great deal
   of trouble because the figures had not been
   proofread. (What caused the trouble?)
   I asked the doctor whether I could see the
   X ray of my brain, and he said it wasn't
   developed. (What wasn't developed?)
   People (not they) say that he is well educated.

4. Nominative-case pronouns, *I, you, he, she, it, they,* or *we,*
should follow linking verbs, *be, being, is, was, am, are, were,
will be, shall be,* and *might be.*

   Examples: This is she speaking.
   That is I.
   Was it he?
   This is he.
   Nobody hinted of its being he.

(Note: In informal conversation, common usage permits saying,
"That's me." and "That's us." In informal conversation use the
words with which you are comfortable. When writing formally,
when addressing groups, or when writing to someone you don't
know, be safe and use the nominative case after linking verbs.)

5. Objective-case pronouns, *me, you, him, her, them, us,* and
whom, are subjects of infinitives.

   Examples: We didn't ask her to do the work.
   The president asked me to serve as acting manager.

6. When the infinitive *to be* does not have a subject of its own and
is followed by a pronoun, the pronoun is in the nominative
case. When the infinitive has a subject of its own, the pronoun
following is in the objective case.

Examples: Would you want to be he?
At a glance I guessed the woman to be her.
Many persons believed it to have been him.
Many persons wanted to have been he.

7. (a)   *Who* or *whoever* is used as a subject or a predicate nominative. If substituting *I, he, she, they,* or *we* makes sense,
use *who.*

Examples: Who is coming?
Give the book to whoever wants it. (*Whoever* is
the subject of *wants,* and *whoever wants it*
is the object of *to.*)

(b)   *Whom* or *whomever* is used as an object. If substituting
me, him, her, them, or *us* makes sense, use *whom.*

Examples: Whom did he call? (He called whom? *Whom* is
the object of *did call.*)
Whom am I to pay for the tickets? (*Whom* is the
object of *to pay.*)

8. *That* is a restrictive pronoun. *Which* is a nonrestrictive pronoun.
That restricts meaning to specific items, and the meaning of the
clause introduced by *that* refers only to those items. *Which*
expresses an incidental thought, and the meaning of the sentence does not change if the clause is omitted. Since nonrestrictive clauses are set off by commas, "which clauses" are
always preceded by commas. When you have a question about
using *that* or *which,* use a comma and *which* if the thought is
incidental to the meaning of the sentence.

Examples: Each building has only two apartments, which
are very small.
(There are only two apartments in each
building. Since the size of the apartments is
incidental to the meaning of the sentence, the
clause is nonrestrictive.)
Each building has only two apartments that are
very small.
(Each building may have many apartments
but only two apartments in each building are
very small. The clause is restrictive since the
meaning of the clause is restricted to only two
apartments.)
Second pages, which are typed on plain sheets of
bond paper, should be labeled to provide
identification.

(This sentence means that all second pages
should be labeled; the clause is nonrestrictive
since the meaning of the clause is not
restricted to any specific second pages.)
Second pages that are typed on plain sheets of
bond paper should be labeled to provide
identification.
(The clause in this sentence is restrictive since
the meaning of the clause is restricted only to
those pages typed on bond paper; pages not
typed on bond paper need not be labeled.)

9. The *self* form of a pronoun should rarely be used; but, when used, *self* must refer to the subject. (There is no such word as *hisself.*)

   Examples: They sent the directions to Mr. Fowler and me
               (not myself).
               He hurt himself.
               Every man must discipline himself.

10. *Them* is not an adjective.

    Example: I do not like those (not them) pens.

11. Pronouns used as adjectives should be in the same case as the nouns they modify.

    Examples: Just among us friends, I plan to resign.
                We girls will decorate the office for the party.

12. *Anybody, everyone, each one, everybody, nobody, someone, somebody, anyone,* and *no one* are singular, so singular pronouns must be used with them.

    Examples: Nobody should go home until he completes his
                work.
                Everyone should always do his best.

13. *That* and *which* are not personal pronouns and should not refer to people.

    Examples: Correct: The employee who resigned accepted
                            a new job.
                Incorrect: The employee that resigned accepted
                            a new job.

Verbs

1. When *s* is added to a verb, the verb becomes singular.

   Examples: *Plural*   *Singular*
              run   runs
              talk   talks
              drive   drives
              laugh   laughs

2. Transitive verbs take objects; intransitive verbs do not. Yet some verbs can be both transitive and intransitive.

   Examples: The secretary sent the papers by registered mail. (Transitive)
              The secretary sent for coffee. (Intransitive)
              We effected the plan last month. (Transitive)
              The president was in New York yesterday. (Intransitive)
              Correct your errors. (Transitive)

3. *Lay* in the present tense is a transitive verb and always has an object.
   Lie is an intransitive verb and never has an object.

   Examples: Lay the book on the table. (Present tense)
              He laid the book on the table yesterday. (Past tense)
              He has laid the book on the table. (Past participle)
              Lie down for a nap. (Present tense)
              Yesterday he lay down for a nap. (Past tense)
              He has lain down for a nap. (Past participle)

4. *Set*, as a transitive verb, always has an object. *Sit* is an intransitive verb and never has an object.

   Examples: Set the vase on the table. (Present tense)
              He set the vase on the table yesterday. (Past tense)
              He has set the vase on the table. (Past participle)

              Sit near the door. (Present tense)
              He sat near the door yesterday. (Past tense)
              He has sat near the door frequently. (Past participle)

   Note: For some specific meanings *set* is an intransitive verb.

   Examples: The sun sets in the west.
              The old hen sets; but, when she sets, she sits on the eggs.

The gelatin sets in an hour.
We set upon our task.

5. *Rise* and *arise* are intransitive verbs and have no objects. *Raise* is a transitive verb and must have an object.

   Examples: The sun rises at seven o'clock.
               I shall arise at 6 a.m.
               The bread rises quickly.
               The boy raised his hand.

6. (a)   *Shall* or *should* usually are used to express future tense with *I* and *we*.
         Will or *would* usually are used to express future tense with *he, she, it, you,* and *they.*

   Examples: I shall leave within an hour.
               He will leave within an hour.
               I should like to leave within an hour.
               He would like to leave within an hour.

   (b)   To express promise or determination, use *will* or *would* with *I* and *we* and *shall* or *should* with *he, she, it, you,* and *they.*

   Examples: I will go regardless of what you say.
               He shall go regardless of what you say.
               I will meet you in an hour.
               He promises that he shall meet us in an hour.

   (c)   *Should* is also used to mean *ought.*

   Examples: I should improve my English.
               He should improve his English.

   (Note: In informal conversation some people use *shall* and *will* interchangeably; but in formal writing or speaking, the words should be used correctly to convey precise meaning.)

7. In the subjunctive mood *were* is used with a singular subject. The subjunctive mood expresses a doubt, an uncertainty, a wish, or something contrary to fact. *Were* is also used in a clause following *as if* or *as though.*

   Examples: If she were late, you should fire her. (She was
                  not late. Subjunctive mood — contrary to fact.)
               If I were she, I'd go soon. (Subjunctive mood —
                  contrary to fact.)
               I wish she were able to do the work.
                  (Subjunctive mood — wish.)
               Were I certain about this, I'd require action.

He acts as if he were guilty.

You speak as though you were an authority.

8. Active voice is usually preferable to passive voice. Often the use of passive voice creates wordiness, is confusing, and is less forceful than active voice.

> Examples: The insurance premium was paid on time by Mr. Jones. (Passive)
>
> Mr. Jones paid the insurance premium on time. (Active)
>
> George was found shot to death by Jim. (Passive. Did Jim shoot George, or did George find Jim?)
>
> Jim found George shot to death. (Active)

9. Present tense should be used for existing things and situations.

> Examples: His name is John. (Not: His name was John. John is alive!)
>
> He told me where the building was. (OK if the building has been moved!)
>
> I asked him where the road was. (Has the road been moved?)
>
> We fished on Blue Lake, which is in Missouri.
>
> What is your name? (Not: What was your name? Of course, if you are asking Mary, a married woman, this question and want to know her maiden name, "What was your name?" would be appropriate.)

Several years ago, at the expense of several million dollars to the taxpayers of the United States, a satellite had to be destroyed at Cape Canaveral shortly after launching simply because a hyphen had been omitted from a set of instructions. Fortunately, not all punctuation errors are so expensive! Some, though, may be quite embarrassing; just misplace a comma or a decimal point in a group of figures and find out!

Punctuation marks are used to assist the reader. A writer doesn't need them, for he should know without punctuation marks what he means. On the other hand, the reader doesn't know what the writer means unless the writer has used appropriate punctuation to give a piece of writing proper pauses, inflections, and separations.

The following rules of punctuation are designed to assist precision of communication. They should become as much a part of a writer as the words he uses.

Apostrophe

1. Use the apostrophe to express the possessive case of nouns. (See "Possessives" under "Grammar Problems," p. 63.)

    Examples: He went on a five months' vacation.
    The men's salaries were increased.
    He got five dollars' worth of change.
    The company's stock was sold privately.

2. Use the apostrophe to show the omission of letters in contractions. Place the apostrophe where the letter or letters are omitted.

    Examples: doesn't for does not
    it's for it is

3. Use the apostrophe to form plurals of letters, numbers, and symbols.

    Examples: the 1970's
    the Oakland A's
    p's and q's
    3's, 5's

4. Use an apostrophe to form the plural of a word referred to as a word.

 Examples: He had three <u>and's</u> in the sentence
 There were five <u>don't's</u> in the paragraph.

5. Use an apostrophe for the plural or some other form of an abbreviation.

 Examples: Two C.O.D.'s were necessary.
 4-H'er

Colon

1. The colon is used after *the following, in the following manner, as follows, thus, this, these,* and similar expressions when they introduce a list or an enumeration.

2. Quotations are often introduced by colons.

 Example: My motto is: "First come, first served."

3. A colon may be used to separate hours from minutes and minutes from seconds.

 Examples: He has a meeting at 9:30 a.m.
 His time for completing the task is 2:25:15.

4. In a bibliography a colon may be used to separate the name of the city of publication from the name of the publisher.

 Example: Simon, Raymond, <u>Public Relations Management:
 Cases & Simulations.</u> Columbus, Ohio:
 Grid, Inc., 1973.

5. A colon is used in references, proportions, Biblical citations, etc.

 Example: Mix the cement, sand, and water for the job in
 the proportion of 1:3:5.

6. Use a colon between the dictator's and the typist's initials at the end of a letter.

 Example: NSJ:mh

7. A colon may follow *attention* and usually follows *subject* when these words are used in attention and subject lines in business letters.

 Examples: Attention: Mr. Harry Barnes
 Subject: Account No. 5031

8. Use a colon after the salutation of a letter if closed or mixed punctuation is used and after the introductory greeting in a typewritten speech.

> Examples: Dear Mr. Gaines:
> Gentlemen:
> Mr. Chairman, Ladies, and Gentlemen:

Comma

1. (a) Words in a series should be separated by commas. A comma is placed before *and* or *or* when one of these words connects the last two items of the series.

> Examples: Please put the letter, the check, and the clipping on my desk.
> Hughes made several assumptions in his conversation with the inspectors, Bill Stone, and Fred Abbott. (Without the comma after *Stone*, *Bill Stone* and *Fred Abbott* would be used in apposition with *inspectors*, meaning that Stone and Abbott are inspectors.)

(b) Do not use a comma when conjunctions connect the series.

> Example: Please bring me the letters and the stamps and the envelopes.

(c) Phrases in a series should be separated by commas.

> Example: The manager wrote to the president, to the secretary, and to the treasurer of the company.

(d) Clauses in a series should be separated by commas. (Clauses containing commas are usually separated by semicolons.)

> Examples: Mr. Ford went to his office, he made several telephone calls, and he wrote many letters that morning.
> If Stanley is still ill, if the highway is icy, or if the car is in the garage, we shall have to change our plans.
> Harold drove to Kansas City, Missouri, on Monday; he flew to Los Angeles, California, on Tuesday; and he sailed for Hawaii on Friday.

(e) When dependent clauses are joined by coordinate conjunctions, no punctuation is placed between those clauses.

Examples: If it rains tomorrow and if the show is canceled, we shall go Thursday.

If the roads are bad or the car is still in the garage tomorrow, we shall have to change our plans. (The meaning of *if* carries over to the second clause.)

(f) If two or more adjectives in a series modify a noun, a comma should separate these adjectives if each adjective modifies the noun alone. (If placing *and* between adjectives in a series makes sense, use a comma between the adjectives.)

Examples: Our cafeteria always serves attractive, well-balanced meals.

He owns a handsome black car.

2. Place a comma between a name and *Jr.*, *Sr.*, *Ltd.*, and *Inc.*

Example: John Smith, Jr.

3. *Yes* or *no* at the beginning of a sentence is followed by a comma.

Example: Yes, we will serve on the committee.

4. A word or words used in addressing a person should be set off by commas.

Examples: Mr. Haller, will you please sign your name on the line marked?

We shall be glad, Mr. Smith, to ship your order tomorrow.

5. An introductory dependent clause is separated by a comma from the independent clause in a sentence. Dependent clauses are introduced by the following subordinate conjunctions:

after	in case that	till
although	in order that	though
as	inasmuch as	unless
as far as	on condition that	until
as if	provided	when
as soon as	since	whenever
as though	so far as	where
because	so that	whereas
before	supposing	wherever
even if	than	whether
how	that	while
if	then	why

Example: If you desire a sample, please write to us soon.

6. A comma separates independent clauses joined by the following coordinate conjunctions:

and	either . . . or	or
but	neither . . . nor	so
for	not only . . . but also	yet

(Note: Do not generalize that commas always precede these conjunctions; see the fourth and fifth examples that follow.)

Examples: Your order arrived today, and we shall send the goods tomorrow.
The committee prepared the rough draft, but Redwood will prepare the revision.
We will not only go to dinner, but we will also go to the movie.
We will not only go to dinner but will also go to the movie.
(This sentence contains one independent clause and a compound predicate.)
We will go not only to dinner but also to the movie.
(This sentence has one independent clause and two prepositional phrases.)

7. A dependent clause within an independent clause must be set off by commas.

Examples: He plans to work tonight; but, if the bus does not run late, he may not finish the report.
He plans, if the bus runs late tonight, to finish the report.

8. (a) A clause expressing a thought that *is not needed* to complete the meaning of the main clause is set off by commas. (A nonrestrictive clause; see *that* and *which*, p. 67.)

Examples: Mr. James Fowler, who manages the Book Department, is ill.
Tom Jones, who met you at the station, is her nephew.

(b) A clause expressing a thought that *is needed* to complete the meaning of the main clause is not set off by commas. (A restrictive clause; see *that* and *which*, p. 67.)

Examples: The file that is near the door is mine.
The boy who met you at the station is her nephew.

9. A comma should follow an introductory verbal phrase.

    Examples: To save time, drive to the bank.
                    The next time we met, Steve had finished his job.

10. Introductory parenthetical words, parenthetical expressions, and mild interjections should be set off by commas.

    Examples: By the way, what date is the deadline?
                    Oh, delivery of the goods next week will be satisfactory.
                    His tardiness, I believe, was caused by the snow.

11. (a) When the following expressions are used parenthetically, they are set off by commas:

after all	in fact
all the same	in other words
as a matter of fact	in short
as a result	in spite of
at least	in the first place
by the way	in the meantime
for all that	of course
for example	on the contrary
for instance	on the other hand
for that reason	on the whole
in addition	that is
in any case	to summarize
in brief	to tell the truth
in conclusion	

    Examples: This was, to tell the truth, rather amusing.
                    We do not know, of course, where he will go.

  (b) Be sure to distinguish between words used parenthetically and the same words used as adjectives or adverbs.

    Examples: However early he arrives at his office, his employer is always there.
                    He arrives at his office early; however, his employer is always there.
                    He arrives, however, on time.

12. If an explanatory phrase or clause breaks into a sentence at any point, it may be set off by commas to preserve the clear continuity of the sentence.

    Example: More snow, along with warmer temperatures, is forecast.

13. A comma is used to set off a question added to a statement.

    Example: The personnel man went to Memphis, did he not?

14. Contrasted expressions are set off by commas.

    Example: It was Miss Casper, not Mr. Casper, who went to the convention.

15. Words in apposition are set off by commas.

    Example: Our salesman, Mr. Ben Jones, called on you.

16. A comma should separate a name and the title or degree that follows.

    Example: Dr. Benson, Dean of the School of Business, made his report.

17. Place a comma before and after *i.e.*, *e.g.*, and *etc.* or *et cetera* except when they end sentences.

    Example: Bring your book, paper, records, etc., to the meeting.

18. Set off direct quotations by commas.

    Example: "I am not interested in your problem," he replied.

19. If a question mark is needed at the end of a quotation, do not use a comma.

    Example: "Is this the lowest price you can quote?" he asked.

20. Always place commas inside quotation marks.

    Example: "If I were there," she said, "I could tell them what to order."

21. Separate the day of the month from the year by a comma. If no day is given, separate the month from the year by a comma. Place a comma after the year if it is not at the end of the sentence.

    Example: Thanksgiving vacation begins November 20, 1974, and ends November 26, 1974.

22. Use a comma to show that one or more words usually understood have been omitted.

    Example: The employer contributed 25 percent; the employees, 25 percent.

23. Use a comma to separate the name of a city from the name of a state. Also place a comma after the state unless it is at the end of a sentence.

    Example: Dickson Company of Omaha, Nebraska, has increased production 50 percent.

24. Use a comma when writing figures in thousands but not numbers of a street, a room, a post-office box, a telephone, an insurance policy, an account, and pages.

    Examples: $13,621.04
    2308 Maine Street
    page 1321

25. A comma is used after the salutation of a personal letter.

    Example: Dear Bill,

26. Use a comma when the meaning would be confused if it were omitted.

    Examples: To Mary, Ann was like a sister.
    To a teacher, chaperoning a class presented many challenges.

27. Expressions starting with the following words placed immediately after the subject of a sentence are set off by commas:

    as well as   consisting of
    assisted by   in addition to
    comprising   together with

    Examples: Mr. Franks, as well as his assistant, will attend the meeting.
    Mr. Lavery, together with his brothers, finished the job in three days.

28. Phrases introduced by the following words and tacked on at the ends of sentences are preceded by commas:

    consisting of   including
    containing   such as
    in addition to

    Examples: Harvey possesses many desirable characteristics, such as dependability, punctuality, and initiative.
    The package contained valuable items, including an expensive suit and a pair of lizard shoes.

29. The following introductory words, when used parenthetically, are set off by commas:

accordingly	indeed	personally
also	likewise	similarly
consequently	meanwhile	still
conversely	moreover	then
finally	naturally	therefore
first, second, etc.	nevertheless	thus
fortunately	next	too
furthermore	normally	unfortunately
hence	now	well
however	obviously	whereas
incidentally	otherwise	yet

Examples: Now, that is not the correct interpretation.
Naturally, immediate action was imperative.

Dash

1. In typewritten work use two hyphens with no space preceding or succeeding them for a dash, or you may use one hyphen preceded by a space and succeeded by a space.

   Examples: word--word
   word - word

2. A dash should rarely be used but may be necessary when there is a sudden break in thought.

   Example: They gave opinions about factors that confront them daily — they gave opinions about themselves.

Ellipsis

1. Use three periods to show an omission of words and use a fourth period or other terminal punctuation mark when the omission ends a sentence.

   Examples: The report said, "We attended . . . trade shows, meetings, and conventions . . . ."
   " . . . a piece of writing is good or bad, effective or ineffective."

2. Three asterisks are used to indicate unprintable words.

   Example: I hope the * * * thing works.

3. Three asterisks are used in the middle of the page to indicate an omission of a paragraph.

   Example: * * *

Exclamation point

1. An exclamation point is placed after expressions of surprise.

   Example: Keep prices down!

2. The exclamation point is sometimes repeated to add emphasis.

    Example: Hurry! Come quickly!

3. Exclamation points, not question marks, follow interrogatory sentences that are exclamatory.

    Example: What difference does it make where he goes!

4. The exclamation mark is placed inside quotation marks when it is part of the quotation.

    Example: They shouted, "Hold that line!"

Hyphen

1. A hyphen is used to divide a word at the end of a line.

2. A hyphen is used between compound numbers below one hundred when they are spelled out.

    Examples: fifty-second
                one hundred thirty-one
                twenty-two

3. A hyphen indicates a time span.

    Example: This period covered the years 1967-1974.

4. Use a hyphen in a compound adjective when it appears before the noun it modifies. (See "Compound adjectives" under "Grammar Problems," p. 56.)

    Examples: a ten-pound turkey
                a thirty-minute drive
                a three-week vacation

5. (a) Fractions used as adjectives are hyphenated. Omit the hyphen between the numerator and the denominator, however, when a hyphen appears in either the numerator or the denominator.

    Examples: a three-fourths turn
                a two-tenths gain
                five one-thousandth inch

   (b) Fractions are hyphenated only when used as adjectives. When a fraction is used as a noun, it is not hyphenated.

    Examples: One half of them went. (noun)
                Make a one-half turn. (adjective)
                Use a 1½-inch strip of metal.
                Use a 1 3/4-inch strip of metal.

6. (a)   The hyphen should be retained in a series of hyphenated words having the same ending.

Examples: first-, second-, and third-class mail
the two- or three-year term

(b)   In a series of hyphenated words following a noun to which the words refer, use a hyphen.

Examples: barrels: 1-gallon, 10-gallon, 50-gallon
stakes: 3-, 4-, 5-inch

7. Some compound words used to represent a single unit of thought are hyphenated.

Examples: father-in-law   a right-of-way
a go-between   a send-off
a know-it-all   a so-and-so
a looker-on   a time-saver
make-believe   a well-wisher

8. Prefixes and suffixes are sometimes hyphenated to root words. Here are some examples of hyphenated prefixes and suffixes; but, when in doubt, check a dictionary.

(a)   *Self* is the only prefix that is always hyphenated before root words.

Examples: self-assured
self-conscious

(b)   All prefixes are hyphenated before capitalized words.

Examples: non-English
un-American

(c)   Prefixes are frequently hyphenated when the prefix ends with a vowel and the root word begins with the same vowel.

Examples: de-emphasis
semi-invalid

(d)   Complete words used as suffixes are often hyphenated to root words, especially when the suffix would cause three identical consonants.

Examples: hull-less
president-elect

(e)   Different meanings may be conveyed by using hyphens after prefixes or before suffixes.

Examples: a fruitless search   a fruit-less diet
             recover the loss   re-cover the chair
             recreate the mind   re-create a situation
             reform a child   re-form the bylaws

9. If a title signifies two offices, it should be hyphenated.

Example: secretary-treasurer

10. Letters used as descriptive words are sometimes hyphenated to
    words to form nouns and are always hyphenated to form adjec-
    tives coming before the nouns they modify.

Examples: 4-H   V-2
             T-shirt   X-radiation
             V-particle   X-axis

Parentheses

1. Use parentheses to set apart parenthetical or explanatory mat-
    ter. Commas or dashes may be used for this purpose, but
    parentheses are stronger marks of punctuation.

Examples: Our convention (to be held in New York this
             year) will honor Mr. Charles Macy for his
             sixty years of service.
             This seems to be the easiest (if not the best)
             method to use.

2. Enclose in parentheses letters or numbers enumerating items in
    context.

Example: The stocks are of two kinds: (1) common stock
            and (2) preferred stock.

3. Parentheses may be used to enclose the dates of a person's life.

Example: John Lang (1880-1960) organized the company.

4. Commas, semicolons, colons, and dashes are outside the paren-
    theses except when punctuating only the parenthetical matter.

Example: It is in many of our contracts (but not in all of
            them); nevertheless, we will agree to the
            proposal.

5. A period, an exclamation point, or a question mark punctuating
    the entire sentence is outside the parentheses. These marks are
    inside the parentheses when punctuating only the parenthetic
    material.

Example: The meeting was held in Washington (D.C.).

6. Continuous parenthetic paragraphs have an opening parenthesis mark before each paragraph but a closing parenthesis after only the last paragraph.

7. Parentheses enclose figures that follow numbers written in words in legal documents.

> Example: I promise to pay fifty dollars ($50).

Period

1. A period should follow each complete sentence unless that sentence is followed by a question mark or an exclamation point.

> Examples: We have offices in the Dwight Building.
> When can you come to Seattle for an
> interview?
> What a busy day we had!

2. Periods are always used after initials and are used after most abbreviations. There is a tendency, however, to omit periods after abbreviations of agencies of the Federal Government and after abbreviations of well-known organizations.

> Examples: FBI
> NEA

3. Do *not* use a period after:
   (a) Headings of chapters, articles, or papers except paragraph headings
   (b) Incomplete statements arranged in tabulated form
   (c) Nicknames, e.g., Bill, Tom
   (d) Contractions, e.g., can't, don't
   (e) The words *ad*, *percent*, and *memo*
   (f) 1st, 2d, 3d
   (g) Roman numerals that are a part of proper names: Louis XIV, Henry VI
   (h) Chemical formulas, e.g., $H_2 O$, $H_2 SO_4$
   (i) Expressions such as OK, IOU, SOS
   (j) Letters identifying radio stations, e.g., KFKU, SX63L
   (k) Sums of money in dollars unless cents are added, e.g., $50, $50.25

4. Place a period after each letter or number in an outline or itemized list unless the letter or the number is enclosed in parentheses.

> Examples: (1)
> 1.
> (a)
> a.

5. Periods should not be used after items in a list unless the items are complete sentences.

6. Place periods inside, never outside, closed quotation marks.

   Examples: He said, "I shall be on time."
               He said, "I shall arrive at 9 a.m."

Question mark

1. Use a question mark at the end of each direct question that requires an answer. Use a period, not a question mark, after an indirect question.

   Examples: How soon will you send the money?
               Has the merchandise been shipped?
               He inquired how the material had been shipped.

2. Do not place a question mark after a question that is a polite request to which no answer is expected.

   Example: Will you please return the copy today.

3. Use the question mark after the individual members of a series, each one of which might be expanded into a complete sentence.

   Examples: Would you guess his age as six? seven? eight?
               How do you like arithmetic? art? typewriting?
               What is the population of Illinois? of Missouri?
               of Nebraska?

4. The question mark should be placed inside the quotation mark when only the quotation is a question. When the whole sentence is a question, the question mark is placed outside the quotation mark.

   Examples: He asked, "Will you go?"
               Did he ask, "Will you go"?

Quotation marks

1. Use quotation marks to enclose the exact words of the speaker. Each part of an interrupted quotation begins and ends with quotation marks. Do not use quotation marks around indirect quotations.

   Examples: "He is not here," she answered.
               "He is not here," she answered, "but I shall find
               him."
               She said she would go.

2. If a quotation consists of several paragraphs, quotation marks should precede each paragraph and should follow only the last

paragraph. Use single quotation marks (') to enclose a quotation within a quotation.

Example: "Then," the speaker continued, "the employer said, 'Excellent,' and approved the report."

3. Quotation marks should enclose word-for-word reproductions of another's writing. Direct quotations need not be preceded by *that*.

Example: I quote the first paragraph of the letter: "Our prices are subject to a discount of 3 percent."

4. Use quotation marks to enclose a word or a phrase accompanied by its definition. (Underscores may be used for the same purpose.)

Example: "Apprise" means to inform.

5. Place quotation marks around a word or a phrase noted as a word or a phrase. (Instead of quotation marks, the underscore may be used.)

Examples: Answer the question with "yes" or "no."
Place the phrase "on Friday" before the date.

6. Quote words used out of the contexts of their usual meanings.

Example: He was "three sheets in the wind" when he arrived at the party.

7. Titles of poems, songs, slogans, pictures, and radio and television programs are enclosed in quotation marks.

Examples: "Silent Night"
"The Song of Hiawatha"

8. Articles from publications and divisions of books and other underscored publications are quoted.

Example: "This Writing Dilemma" appears in Personnel Journal.

9. When a quotation mark and another mark of punctuation occur together, apply the following rules.

(a)   Place the period or the comma *always inside* the quotation mark.

Examples: He quoted an article entitled "The Cost of War."
After he quoted the article, "Learn Thyself,"
the meeting adjourned.

(b) Place the colon or the semicolon *always outside* the quotation mark.

    Examples: He writes under the head of "Prices": "The index will rise higher."

                  Sanderson speaks of "improving markets"; however, improvement will be delayed until next year.

(c) Question marks and exclamation points come before or after the quotation marks, depending upon the meaning of the text.

    Examples: Who is the author of "The Black Cottage"?
                  He shouted, "I will never apologize for that!"

Semicolon

1. A semicolon is used to separate the parts of a compound sentence when there is no conjunction.

    Example: The adjustment has been made; the case has been closed.

2. Use a semicolon to separate clauses that contain commas.

    Examples: You may study long; but, if you do not concentrate on your lessons, you will not learn much.

                  Some people confuse their, the personal pronoun; there, the adverb; and they're, the contraction.

3. In enumerations use semicolons to separate the items unless they are short and simple, also to separate items that contain commas.

    Example: The following people enrolled: Mary Smith, Concordia; Tom Lardner, New York; and Donna Jones, Portland.

4. Use a semicolon between independent clauses joined by the following words: (Use commas after these words if they are used as connectives.)

accordingly	finally	indeed
also	first	likewise
apparently	fortunately	meanwhile
besides	furthermore	moreover
consequently	hence	namely
conversely	however	naturally
else	incidentally	nevertheless

next	personally	thence
notwithstanding	secondly	theoretically
now	similarly	therefore
obviously	still	thus
otherwise	then	yet

Examples: This is the plan; however, we may vote to
change it.
We have devised a plan; however good or bad it
might be, we shall use it.

5. A semicolon is used before an abbreviation or a word that in-
troduces a long enumeration or a list of items in a sentence. A
comma is placed after the word. Such abbreviations and words
are *e.g.*, *i.e.*, *for example, namely, to wit, etc.*

Example: There is more than one way to make an
exclamation mark; for example, one can be
made by holding down the space bar and
hitting the period and the apostrophe.

Underscore

1. Titles of books, plays, magazines, newspapers, monographs,
operas, musical comedies, booklets, and manuscripts are underscored. Occasionally such titles are written in all capital letters.

Examples: <u>Office Management</u> is a valuable reference book.
<u>Summer and Smoke</u> will be given next week.
<u>South Pacific</u> will be the last performance of the
season.
<u>The Saturday Evening Post</u> was a weekly
magazine.
<u>The Kansas City Star</u> is an evening newspaper.

2. Foreign words and stressed words are underscored.

Examples: She gave her <u>au revoir</u> and left the room.
This simple job should not require <u>four</u>
months of training.

(Note: Some foreign words and expressions have become so
commonly used in English that they are no longer considered
foreign and, consequently, need not be underscored, e.g., vice
versa.)

Careful writers seldom use abbreviations except those that are extremely common and generally accepted for specific reference. Some of the most common abbreviations have more than one meaning. *U.S.A.*, for example, can stand for *United States of America* and for *United States Army*. Because of several meanings for some abbreviations and the resulting possibilities of misinterpretation, abbreviations should be used sparingly.

Proper names (e.g., *Geo.* for *George* and *Wm.* for *William*) are never abbreviated unless the possessors of the names abbreviate them. Likewise, initials are never substituted for proper names unless the possessors use them.

Abbreviations of armed-forces rank designations and civilian titles are acceptable before and after names. When names are given, use the abbreviations specified by the possessors of the ranks or the titles. However, in context, when names are not used, spell rank designations and titles in full.

Governmental agencies and private associations may be abbreviated as the agencies abbreviate them.

The following lists contain abbreviations that are acceptable:

Acceptable abbreviations	Meaning
A.D.	Anno Domini
a.m., A.M.	until 12 noon (ante meridiem)
AM	amplitude modulation
B.C.	before Christ
B.T.U., B.t.u., Btu.	British Thermal Unit
C.	centigrade
C.D.T., CDT	central daylight time
c.o.d., C.O.D.	collect on delivery
C.P.A.	Certified Public Accountant
C.P.S.	Certified Professional Secretary
C.S.T., CST	central standard time
cwt.	hundredweight
D.C.	District of Columbia
Dr.	doctor
D.T.	daylight time
E.D.T., EDT	eastern daylight time
e.g.	for example (exempli gratia)
E.S.T., EST	eastern standard time

F.	Fahrenheit
F.B.M., fbm, f.b.m.	feet board measure
Fig(s)., fig(s).	figure(s)
FM	frequency modulation (radio)
f.o.b., F.O.B.	free on board
G.C.T., GCT	Greenwich civil time
GMAT	Greenwich mean astronomical time
G.M.T., GMT	Greenwich mean time
GNP	gross national product
Gov.	Governor
G.S.T., GST	Greenwich sidereal time
H.M.S., HMS	His, or Her, Majesty's Ship or Service
Hon.	Honorable
H.T., HT	Hawaiian Time
i.e.	that is (id est)
I.Q.	intelligence quotient
M.D.T., MDT	mountain daylight time
Messrs.	Messieurs, Misters
Mr.	Mister
Mrs. (Mmes.)	Mistress (Mesdames)
Ms.	Miss, Mrs. (Use according to the preference of the reader or when marital status is unknown.)
M.T., MT	mountain time
N.G.	National Guard
p., pp.	page, pages
P.D.T., PDT	Pacific daylight time
p.m., P.M.	after 12 noon (post meridiem)
P.S.	postscript
P.T., PT	Pacific time
Rev.	Reverend
R.F.D.	rural free delivery
R.R.	railroad, rural route
R.S.V.P.	reply if you please
sic.	thus (confirms a word that might be questioned)
SOS	distress signal of ships
S.S., SS	streamship
St.	Saint
TNT	trinitrotoluene
U.S.	United States
U.S.A.	United States of America, United States Army
vol., vols.	volume, volumes

Permissible abbreviations (but not recommended)	Meanings
A.P., A/P	accounts payable
bbl.	barrel, barrels
b/l	bill of lading
bu.	bushel, bushels
cc, c.c.	carbon copy
C/O	care of
Co.	company (*Co.* is used only when a part of an official company name.)
Corp.	corporation (*Corp.* is used only when a part of an official company name.)
ct.	cent
cu.	cubic
D.C.	District Court
Esq.	Esquire
et al.	and others (et alii)
etc.	and so forth (et cetera)
ft.	foot, feet
gal.	gallon, gallons
gr.	gram, gross, grade
h.f., HF	high frequency
hp., hp. HP	horsepower
hp -hr.	horsepower-hour
in., ins.	inch, inches
Inc.	Incorporated (*Inc.* is used only when a part of an official company name.)
lb., lbs.	pound, pounds
Ltd.	Limited (*Ltd.* is used only when a part of an official company name.)
N/30	net 30 days
N.E.	Northeast
No.	Number
N.W.	Northwest
o	degrees
oz.	ounce, ounces
pt., pts.	pint, pints
qt., qts.,	quart, quarts
S.E.	Southeast
S.W.	Southwest
yd., yds.	yard, yards

See abbreviations used in footnotes, pp. 31.

Abbreviations of states and territories

Although spelling the names of states and territories in full in letters and on envelopes maximizes clarity and accuracy, the Post Office Department approves the following abbreviations to be used with Zip Codes only:

Alaska	AK	Montana	MT
Alabama	AL	Nebraska	NB
Arizona	AZ	Nevada	NV
Arkansas	AR	New Hampshire	NH
California	CA	New Jersey	NJ
Canal Zone	CZ	New Mexico	NM
Colorado	CO	New York	NY
Connecticut	CT	North Carolina	NC
Delaware	DE	North Dakota	ND
District of Columbia	DC	Ohio	OH
Florida	FL	Oklahoma	OK
Georgia	GA	Oregon	OR
Hawaii	HI	Pennsylvania	PA
Idaho	ID	Puerto Rico	PR
Illinois	IL	Rhode Island	RI
Indiana	IN	South Carolina	SC
Iowa	IA	South Dakota	SD
Kansas	KS	Tennessee	TN
Kentucky	KY	Texas	TX
Louisiana	LA	Utah	UT
Maine	ME	Vermont	VT
Maryland	MD	Virginia	VA
Massachusetts	MA	Virgin Islands	VI
Michigan	MI	Washington	WA
Minnesota	MN	West Virginia	WV
Mississippi	MS	Wisconsin	WI
Missouri	MO	Wyoming	WY

The general rule for capitalizing the first letter of a word is to capitalize all proper nouns, that is, items that have been named to distinguish them from other like items. Newspapers and magazines tend to capitalize as few words as possible; however, for other types of writing the following illustrations provide a comprehensive set of examples for capitalization.

Academic-degree abbreviations and initial designations

    Examples: Alvin C. Jones, M.D.
                  John Brown, Ph.D.
                  Keith Jackson, C.P.A.
                  Harold Krow, C.L.U.

Airplanes, railroads, trains, and steamships

    Examples: Boeing 747
                  Ambassador Flight
                  Union Pacific
                  City of St. Louis
                  Queen Mary

Astronomical bodies

    Examples: Mars
                  Venus
                  Earth
                  Big Dipper
                  North Star

Books, magazines, newspapers, musical compositions, manuscripts, and poems

In titles capitalize the first word and all other words except articles, conjunctions, and short prepositions.

    Examples: Gone with the Wind
                  Time
                  The Kansas City Star
                  "Home on the Range"
                  "The Duel"

Brand and trade names

> Examples: Corningware
> Vel
> Tide
> Bon Ami

Churches and derived names

> Examples: First Methodist Church
> Presbyterian Church
> Catholics
> Baptists

Clubs and their members

> Examples: Chamber of Commerce
> Veterans of Foreign Wars
> a Mason
> an Elk

Company, institutional, and organizational names and their departments

> Examples: H. L. Seevers, Inc.
> National Publishing Company
> International Business Machines
> Sunnyvale Old Folks Home
> Purchasing Department, ABC Company
> Sales Department, YXW Company

Deity and books of the Bible

> Examples: Father
> God
> Lord
> Almighty
> Jehovah
> Savior
> Thee
> Thou
> He
> Deuteronomy

Derivatives of proper nouns are not always capitalized (Check a dictionary.)

> Examples: American plan   china (dishes)
> americanize   derby (hat)
> anglicize   french (to cut)
> bohemian   french fries
> boycott   homburg (hat)

india ink   oxfords (shoes)
italic   pasteurize
japan (varnish)   plaster of paris
jersey (cloth)   platonic
kelly joint   scotch (crush)

Kelly green   Scotch broth
macadam   sweet william
manila (paper)   watt
morocco (leather)

Directions only when they refer to sections of the country

Examples: south of town
east of the bridge
the North
Middle West
Midwest
the South
Southern accent
an Easterner

Geographic names, rivers, lakes, and parks

Examples: Missouri River
Atlantic Ocean
Rocky Mountains
the West Coast
the Coast
Lone Star Lake
the Tropics
Yellowstone Park

Governmental bodies

Examples: Senate
House
Congress
Cabinet
Bureau of the Census
Civil Service Commission
Supreme Court of the United States
Colorado Supreme Court
Illinois Legislature
United States Navy

Governor used before the name of a state

Examples: the Governor of Indiana
the Governor of Kentucky
the governors of Florida, Idaho, and Missouri

Headings

Type titles of chapters and main divisions of reports in upper-case letters. Capitalize only the first letter of the first word and of important words in center-page headings. Capitalize the first letter of the first word of marginal and paragraph headings. The first letter of important words of marginal and paragraph headings may be capitalized but need not be. However, be consistent within each type of heading.

Examples: <u>Fear of Making Mistakes</u> (or) <u>Fear of making mistakes</u>
             <u>Writing Mechanics</u>   (or) <u>Writing mechanics</u>

Historic events

Examples: World War I
             Spanish-American War
             the Revolutionary War
             the Renaissance

Holidays

Examples: Thanksgiving
             Christmas
             Easter
             Independence Day, the Fourth of July

Hyphenated words

Capitalize only proper nouns and the first letter of hyphenated words.

Examples: un-American
             Sixty-three
             One Hundred Forty-eight (as on checks)
             English-speaking people

Laws

Examples: Social Security Act
             Public Law 316
             Labor Management Relations Act of 1947

Months and Days of the Week

Examples: Tuesday, January 1
             Saturday, March 23

Nations, nationalities, and languages

Examples: Chinese   Spanish
             Caucasian   France
             Latin.

Outlines

Capitalize the first letter of the first word of each line only.

Example: Parts of a business letter
    A.   Date
    B.   Inside address
        1. Individual's name
        2. Company's name
        3. Street address
        4. City and state
        5. Zip number
    C.   Salutation

Phrases or sentences following a colon

Example: Here is the reason he gave: His car arrived late.

Poetry

Capitalize the first word of each line. Some authors, particularly when writing free verse, do not capitalize the first word of each line. In such cases, use the style the author uses.

Examples: Mary had a little lamb
          Its fleece was white as snow.

          The wind blew strong
          on yonder hill

Political parties and factions

Examples: Democrat
          Republican
          Socialist

Proper names

Examples: John Doe
          New York
          President Washington
          Senator Carlson

Quotations

Capitalize the first letter of the first word in quotations.

Examples: The clerk said, "The tax is 53 cents."
          Ask yourself, "Can I afford to be without the appliance?"

Resolutions

Capitalize the first letter of the first word following *Whereas* or *Resolved* in resolutions.

> Examples: Whereas, It is important . . .
> Resolved, That the meeting . . .

Salutations and complimentary closes

In salutations capitalize only the first letter of the first word and words representing people addressed. Capitalize only the first word of a complimentary close.

> Examples: Dear Mr. Norris
> My dear Mr. Haynes
> To the Heads of Departments
> Sincerely yours
> Very sincerely yours

School subjects

Capitalize the first letter of each word in school subjects that are derived from proper nouns and school subjects that denote specific courses at specific institutions.

> Examples: English
> Spanish
> He is taking psychology, English, and botany.
> He enrolled in General Psychology and
> Introductory Economics at the University of
> Oregon.

Schools, colleges, and their departments

> Examples: School of Business, The University of Arizona
> Grinnell College
> West Junior High School
> Anatomy Department, the State University of
> Connecticut

Seasons

Capitalize seasons only when personified.

> Examples: spring
> summer
> autumn
> fall
> winter
> Old Man Winter

Sentences

Capitalize the first letter of the first word of every sentence.

Examples: The office is closed.
Where is he employed?

Shortened references to specific proper nouns and names

Examples: the Army, the Navy, and the Air Force
the Union
the Government
Federal
the Constitution

the University
the State
the Senate
the House
Department

Company
the Governor
the Mayor
the Chancellor
the President

Streets, highways, and buildings

Examples: Third Street
Main Street
Dwight Building
Lincoln Highway
Grand Army of the Republic Highway
Avenue of the Americas
Route 66
Interstate 75

Tabulated lists

Capitalize the first letter of the first word of each line in tabulated lists.

Examples: The new regulation specifies the following policies:

1. Hours worked
2. Vacation periods
3. Sick leave

Titles

Before and after names capitalize the first letter of each important word in titles denoting high-level positions.

Examples: Dean Smith

President Owens
Captain Jones
Governor Johnson
Chief Justice Burger

Dr. James Smith, Professor of Business
John Owens, President, ABC Company
Chancellor Green
Mary Smith, typist
laborer Jones

Words used as names

Examples:　Did Father work late last night?
Call Uncle Fred when you arrive.

Words written before figures and letters

Except for *page*, *note*, *line*, and *verse*, capitalize the first letter of a word that comes before figures and letters.

Examples:　Table 5
Figure 3
Chapter 7
Appendix A
Exhibit 1

Room 110
Apartment 304
page 423
line 28
verse four

NUMBER STYLE

Most rules for writing numbers have exceptions, but a writer should remember the reader when writing numbers. If a figure is easier to grasp than a word, use a figure. Conversely, if a word is easier to grasp than a figure, use a word. However, as a general guide, follow these rules:

1. Use figures for all numbers above ten. In a series of numbers, if some are below ten and some above ten, use figures for all of them.

    Example: 35 boxes, 4 bales, and 12 lugs

2. A hyphen is used between compound numbers when they are spelled out.

    Examples: thirty-six
                one hundred twenty-three (not one hundred
                    and twenty three)

3. Never use numbers as substitutes for months.

    Example: September 1, 1974 (not 9/1/74 or 9-1-74)

4. When *o'clock* is used, always spell out the time of day. If *a.m.* or *p.m.* is used, use figures.

    Examples: Nine o'clock
                9 p.m.
                9:43 a.m.
                9:30 (If clearly understood, *a.m.* or *p.m.* may be
                    omitted after hours *and* minutes.)

5. Spell out common fractions in isolated cases; if a fraction appears with whole numbers, use figures.

    Examples: One third of the debt was paid.
                We bought 1 1/2 tons of coal.

6. When two numbers appear together in a sentence, write in full the smaller one. Separate numbers in a series by commas.

    Examples: There are twelve 25's in the column.
                The article appears on pages 9, 10, 11, and 12.

7. Avoid using a number at the beginning of a sentence. When a number is the first word, it should be spelled in full.

   Examples: A new era began in 1492 (Not: 1492 marked a new era.)
   Fifteen hundred people attended the convention. (Not: 1,500 people attended the convention.)

8. Use figures for sums of money.

   Examples: $1 (No ciphers, no decimal)
   63 cents (no decimal)
   $1.50
   $5 million

9. Use figures to express ratios.

   Examples: The odds were 2-to-1 in his favor.
   The assets were 5-to-2 over liabilities.

10. Express house numbers in figures except for house number *One*.

    Examples: One Park Avenue
    2 Park Avenue

11. Days are written in figures. Use *st.*, *d*, or *th* only when the day precedes the month. Spell out *first* when referring to the first part of the month.

    Examples: March 23, 1925,
    23rd of March, 1925,
    the first of January, 1974,
    1 January 1974 (Military style. Commas are omitted.)

12. In context do not run figures together in a long number without the appropriate dividing commas. (Exceptions: serial numbers, policy numbers, house numbers, Zip Codes, and numbers of post-office boxes, rooms, streets, telephones, years, and pages.)

    Examples: 1,362,542 (Not: 1362542)
    1,587 (Not: 1587)
    1500 (if pronounced *fifteen hundred*)
    6,000,000 or 6 million (Not: 6000000)
    1,587 cows and 1,500 sheep (Be consistent; use comma even though pronounced *fifteen hundred*.)

13. Except for *$*, spell out symbols in context.

    Examples: $72 (Not: 72 dollars)

35 cents (Not: 35¢)
72 degrees (Not: 72°)
17 inches (Not: 17")
4 by 6 inches (Not: 4" x 6" or 4 x 6")
6 percent (Not: 6%)

(Note: In technical papers containing many measurements, symbols are permitted. But be consistent!)

14. *No.* may be used with figures but never with the word *number* written out. Do not use *#* for *number* except for stock or serial numbers and specifications.

Examples: No. 623 (Not: Number 623)
Box 456 (Not: Box No. 456)
Room 932 (Not: Room No. 932)
Typewriter # 12345

15. Express plurals of figures by adding *'s*.

Example: 16's

16. Columns of Arabic or Roman numerals are aligned on the right or over a decimal point.

Examples:	I	6,392	7,321.62
	II	135	43.766
	III	29	38,942.7
	IV	3	.531

17. In legal documents, specifications, and bids spell out numbers followed by figures in parentheses.

Example: Five hundred thirty-two dollars ($532.00)

18. Approximations are usually spelled out; however, qualifying adverbs, such as *about, around, nearly, almost,* express approximations clearly.

Examples: a thousand
several hundred
fifty people
about 50 people

The first rule of word division is: *Do not divide words at the ends of typewritten lines.* But, if you divide words, divide them only when necessary and observe the following rules that have been designed to aid readability. After reading the rules, you will be convinced that words should not be divided.

No set of rules for dividing words is infallible. For example, *prescience* cannot be divided without violating at least one of the rules. On the other hand, by blindly observing the rules, readability can be impaired, a high price to pay for an even right margin. For example, in each of the following cases, the correct pronunciation of the first part of the division depends upon the last part; readability, therefore, is impaired.

labo-	ratory	rious
hypo-	crite	dermic
mat-	ing	ter
plac-	ing	oid
mar-	ried	ket
reduc-	ing	tase
nec-	essary	tar
mag-	istrate	nanimous
noto-	rious	riety
homo-	nym	genize
mole-	cule	hill
memo-	rial	randum
lino-	leum	type
mean-	der	ing
prob-	lem	ing
din-	ing	ner
min-	ing	eral
hide-	ous	bound
hid-	ing	den
stat-	ing	ute
typ-	ical	ist
log-	ical	book

If words must be divided at the ends of typewritten lines, then follow these rules:

A.   1. Divide a word between syllables only. Pronounce the word
with care to identify the syllables and check a dictionary when
in slightest doubt.

> Examples: pre-serve, pres-er-va-tion, steno-graphic,
>   ste-nog-ra-phy

2. Words of one syllable must not be divided.

> Examples: thought, through, straight, searched, planned

3. Never separate a single-letter syllable at the beginning or at
the end of a word.

> Examples: about, among, piano, steady

4. Never separate a two-letter syllable at the end of a word,
and avoid (if possible) separating a two-letter syllable at
the beginning of a word.

> Examples: delighted, wanted

B.   Put on the first line enough of the word to be divided to suggest
what the completed word will be.

> Example: counsel-ling (not coun-selling)

C.   When a word containing three or more syllables is to be divided
at a one-letter syllable, do one of the following things:

1. For most words write the one-letter syllable on the first
line.

> Examples: sepa-rate, regu-late

2. For words to be divided at a point where two vowels that
are pronounced separately come together, divide the word
between the one-letter syllables.

> Examples: gradu-ation, avi-ation

D.   Divide hyphenated words only at the hyphen.

> Example: self-supporting

E.   Divide prefixes and suffixes of three or more letters as follows:

1. Divide after the prefix and before the suffix.

> Examples: anti-trust, dis-appear, over-turn, trans-late,
>   sub-sist, gor-geous, ten-sion, ambi-tion,
>   atten-tive, expan-sive

2. Two-syllable suffixes, *able*, *ible*, *ical*, are divided after the *a*
or *i* when these letters are pronounced with the preceding
syllables or when awkward divisions result.

Examples:	verita-ble	(not verit-able)
	legi-ble	(not leg-ible)
	logi-cal	(not log-ical)
	techni-cal	(not techn-ical)
	work-able	(not worka-ble)
	resist-ible	(not resisti-ble)
	med-ical	(not medi-cal)

3. When a suffix is added to a word that ends in a double consonant, divide between the second consonant and the suffix.

Examples: fill-ing, full-ness

4. When a word ends in a single consonant and the consonant is doubled when adding a suffix, divide between the double consonants.

Examples: begin-ning, plot-ting

F.   Do not divide:
 1. Abbreviations
 2. Contractions
 3. Figures
 4. Last word in a paragraph
 5. Last word on a page
 6. Month from the day
 7. Words with fewer than five letters

G.   Avoid dividing:
 1. Cities from states
 2. Initials from surnames
 3. Proper nouns
 4. Titles from names
 5. Units of measure from preceding figures
 6. Words at the ends of three or more successive lines
 7. Words at the ends of the first lines of the bodies of letters
 8. Words at the ends of the last lines of the bodies of letters
 9. Year from day or month

H.   Do not divide words in a way that may distract the reader's attention from the context.

Examples:	bar-gain	later-ally
	devel-opment	male-factor
	ear-nest	man-goes
	even-tual	mate-rial
	furn-ace	men-ace
	hot-test	mes-sage

nov-ice   rear-range
read-just   rein-statement
reap-pear   sour-ces

Because of similar pronunciations or inexact usage, many words are confused or are used imprecisely. This section is designed to clarify confusing words and to assist writers achieve precise communication.

A is used before all consonants except silent *H*.
An is used before all vowels except long *U*.

> Examples: A horse   An honor
>   A union   An hour

A and *an* are indefinite articles and are never used with plural words. *The* is a definite article and may be used with singular or plural words. With plural words often an article is not needed. In an indefinite sense an article is not used when the noun is plural.

> Examples: Give him an apple (any apple).
>   Give him the apple you have (specific apple).
>   Buy her a typewriter (any typewriter).
>   Buy her the typewriter you saw today (specific typewriter).
>   In these examples use hyphens before root words.
>   Place apostrophes correctly in the following words.
>   We moved chairs into the room.
>   We moved the chairs into the room.

A should not be used for *of*.

> Examples: What time of (not *a*) night is it?
>   That kind of (not *a*) material is strong.

A while is an article followed by a noun.
Awhile is an adverb.

> Examples: For a while the solution to the problem
>   seemed difficult.
>   The fire alarm sounded awhile ago.

About and *around* mean on all sides and should not be used for *nearly*, *almost*, or *throughout;* nor should *about* and *around* be used in the same expression.

> Examples: It is nearly (not *around* or *about*) five o'clock.

We walked throughout (not *around* and *about*) the
building.

Accede means to approve or to agree.
  Exceed means going past a limit.

    Examples: He acceded to their demands.
                      The car exceeded the speed limit.

Accent means emphasis.
  Ascend means to move upward.
  Assent means agreement or consent.

    Examples: Place an accent mark on the second syllable.
                      Mr. Moore ascended to the presidency of the
company.
                      He assented to the idea after an explanation was
made.

Accept is a verb.
  Except is a preposition indicating an exclusion.

    Examples: He will accept the position.
                      Everyone except Charles was in the office.

Access is a means of approach.
  Excess means something extra and should not be used to mean
additional.

    Examples: He has access to the new library for his research.
                      We have an excess of free literature.
                      My additional (not *excess*) income will be invested
in stocks.

Accidentally is commonly misspelled *accidently*.
Ad means advertisement.
  Add is a verb meaning to join or to unite.

    Examples: He ran the ad in the paper several times.
                      We shall add another department to the business
this year.

Adapt means to adjust.
  Adept refers to skill or aptitude.
  Adopt means to accept.

    Examples: We must adapt ourselves to new ways of living.
                      He is adept at operating the machines.
                      We shall adopt new procedures in the factory.

Add — See *Ad.*

Addenda are things added to a completed work.

Agenda is a plan for a meeting.

Examples: We shall place the new names in the addenda of
the directory.
How many items are on the agenda for the
board meeting?

Adept — See *Adapt*.

Admit — See *Confess*.

Admission is the fee paid for entering a place or the granting of a
position not fully proved.

Admittance is permission to enter a building or a locality.

Examples: The admission to the movie is $1.
Admission of his guilt was unexpected.
Tom secured admittance to the restricted area.

Adopt — See *Adapt*.

Adverse means acting against.

Averse means having a dislike or being unwilling.

Divers means various.

Diverse means different or opposing.

Inverse means opposite in order.

Examples: The plane encountered adverse winds.
That group is averse to war.
Try divers methods while working on that
project.
The committee members held diverse opinions.
The items were arranged in inverse order.

Advice is a noun.

Advise is a verb and means to give advice and does not mean to
tell.

Examples: The superintendent gave him good advice.
Did you advise Bob to continue his education?
Please tell (not *advise*) me when the order will be
shipped.

Affect is a verb and means to influence. *Affectation* is the noun
form.

Effect is usually a noun; however, it may be a verb when it means
to bring about.

Examples: Did that heat affect your health?
What effect did the ruling have on your business?
The committee effected (brought about) a change
early last year.

Age should not be used for *ages* or *aged*.

Examples: They have two children, aged (or ages but not age) seven and nine.
They have one child, age six.

Agenda — See *Addenda.*
Aggravate means to make worse.
Annoy means to disturb or to bother.
Irritate is a stronger word than *annoy* and means to excite to impatience or anger.

Examples: His frequent tardiness annoys the employer.
The long trip aggravated her malady.
His griping irritates me.

Aim should not be used for *intend.*

Example: I intend (not *aim*) to be on time.

All and *both* are used correctly before nouns.
All of and *both of* are used correctly before pronouns.

Examples: All men will attend the meeting.
Both men will attend the meeting.
All of you may attend the meeting.
Both of you may attend the meeting.

All ready means that everything is ready.
Already is an adverb meaning previously.

Examples: The presents were all ready to be sent.
She has already left the office.

All right, according to *Webster's New Collegiate Dictionary,* may be written as one or two words; however, use the form appropriate for most readers — *all right.*

Example: Everything is all right.

All together means all things are together in one place.
Altogether means entirely or wholly.

Examples: The pages are all together on my desk.
They are altogether too heavy.

All ways means in every way.
Always means on every occasion or at all times.

Examples: Miss Jones tried in all ways to please her boss.
Miss Jones is always present.

Aloud means spoken. (See *Out loud.*)
Allowed means permitted.

Examples: He read the poem aloud.
            He allowed two yards of material for shrinkage.

Allusion is an indirect reference.
   Delusion is a fixed misconception arising from a disturbed mind.
   Illusion is a deceptive appearance or a false impression.

Examples: He made no allusions to her peculiarities.
            He operates under the delusion that everyone
            opposes him.
            The illusion of moisture on the street was noticed
            by many.

Almost — See *More, Practically,* and *About.*
Altogether — See *All together.*
Always — See *All ways.*
Among is used when referring to three or more things.
   Between is used when referring to two things.

Examples: The student had to choose between chemistry and
            physics.
            The profits were divided among the many
            stockholders.

Amount expresses general quantity.
   Number expresses countable units.

Examples: The amount of rainfall was small.
            The number attending the concert was large.

And etc. should not be used together. *Etc.* is an abbreviation for the
   Latin *et cetera. Et* is the Latin for *and,* so *and* before *etc.* is
   redundant. *Etc.* is always preceded by a comma.
Anecdote means a clever or an interesting incident or a joke.
   Antidote means a remedy to counteract something.

Examples: The speaker told an anecdote about his childhood.
            Vinegar is an antidote for lye.

Angel means a spiritual being.
   Angle means a geometric form.

Examples: Mary played the role of an angel in the
            Christmas program.
            A square has four right angles.

Angry is an adjective expressing unhappiness or displeasure.
   Mad means insane.

Examples: He was angry because he failed the examination.
            In the park we saw a mad dog.

Annals are records.
  Annual means yearly.
  Annul means to cancel.

  Examples: This month is one of the hottest in the city's
              annals.
              The president's annual salary is $100,000.
              The board members are attempting to annul the
              decision of the president.

Annoy — See *Aggravate*.
Annual — See *Annals*.
Annul — See *Annals*.
Anti is hyphenated only before capital letters.

  Examples: anti-Semite
              antidote
              antislavery

Anticipate means to foresee.
  Expect means to await an outcome.
  Suppose means to assume. (See *Figure* and *Calculate*.)

  Examples: The company anticipates increased profits.
              The president expects to arrive there today.
              I suppose the change will be beneficial.

Antidote — See *Anecdote*.
Anxious denotes concern, anxiety, apprehension, or dread.
  Eager expresses interest or keen desire.

  Examples: I am anxious about my sick brother.
              Aren't you eager to get back to work?

  (Note: Colloquially, *eager* is so often associated with *beaver*
  that *eager* is frequently avoided in writing.)

Any one is an adjective modifying a noun and means any item or
person.
  Anyone is a personal pronoun and means no particular one.

  Examples: Any one of the machines will be satisfactory.
              Any one of you may go.
              Anyone can use this machine.

Any time is always two words.
Any way is the noun *way* limited by the adjective *any*.
  Anyway means anyhow or in any case.

  Examples: Can we help the situation in any way?
              Anyway, we can't depend on him.

Anyone — See *Any one.*

Anyway — See *Any way.*

Anywheres is not an acceptable word and should not be used for *anywhere.*

Apportion means divide.

   Proportion means a share.

     Examples: The increases were apportioned according to merit.

                 What proportion of the work was done by the chairman?

Appraise means to evaluate the worth of something.

   Apprise means to inform.

     Examples: Did he appraise the property?

                 He will apprise all members of the meeting date.

Appreciate is an intransitive verb only when it refers to increase of value.

     Examples: Land values will appreciate during the next five years. (Intransitive, no object.)

                 I appreciate your opinion. (Transitive, object.)

Apprise — See *Appraise.*

Approve means to have a favorable opinion.

   Endorse means to approve in writing or to support.

     Examples: The committee approved his recommendation.

                 He endorsed the note.

                 The party will endorse the candidate.

Apt refers to natural ability, aptitude, or quickness to learn.

   Liable means responsible or obliged by law.

   Libel is a statement harming one's reputation.

   Likely means probably.

     Examples: She is an apt student.

                 Mr. Turney is liable for that debt.

                 He was sued for libel.

                 The forecaster says that Texas is likely to have rain.

Arise — See *Arise,* p. 70.

Around — See *About.*

Arraign means to bring charges in court.

   Arrange means to place in order.

     Examples: The prisoner was arraigned in district court.

The secretary arranged the names in alphabetical order.

As is inappropriate in the sense of *whether* or *that*.

Example: I do not know whether (not *as*) I will go.

As if — See *Like*.
Ascend — See *Accent*.
Assent — See *Accent*.
Assistance is the act of aiding.
  Assistants are helpers.

Examples: Ask Mr. Jones for assistance.
              The head of the department has two assistants.

Aught is a cipher.
  Ought is a verb expressing obligation.

Examples: How many aughts are in your telephone number?
              He did not know what he ought to do.

Averse — See *Adverse*.
Avocation is something done in addition to an occupation.
  Vocation is the making of a living in a business or a profession.

Examples: Collecting stamps is his avocation.
              Teaching history is his vocation.

Awful and *awfully* provide negative connotations and should not be used in the positive sense.

Example: The pie was especially (not *awfully*) good.

Awhile — See *A while*.
Bad is an adjective and, consequently, describes nouns and pronouns.
  Badly is an adverb and, consequently, describes verbs and adjectives.

Examples: We received a bad shipment of parts.
              He is bad.
              The machine runs badly.
              That is a badly managed company.

Balance should not be used for *remainder* or *rest*.

Examples: The rest (not *balance*) of the books may be
                  discarded.
              Do you know the balance of your bank account?

Baring means uncovering.
  Barring means excluding.

Bearing means carrying.

Examples: Baring the facts, he discovered a logical solution.
Barring bad weather, we shall be there.
He is bearing the burden of being a convict.

Beau — See *Bow.*
Because of — See *Due to.*
Berth means place, part, position, or billet.
Birth refers to the bearing of offspring or a beginning.

Examples: The ship was guided into its berth by a tugboat.
The kingdom celebrated the birth of the prince.
The birth of our nation was in 1776.

Beside means by the side of or not included in.
Besides means in addition.

Examples: He sat beside Mr. Jones at the dinner.
Besides our family, ten were present.

Better is used to compare two persons or things.
Best is used to compare more than two persons or things.

Examples: She types better than her assistant.
She is the best typist in the office.

Between — See *Among.*
Biannual means twice a year.
Biennial means once in two years.
Bimonthly means twice a month or every two months.
Biweekly means twice a week or every two weeks.
Biyearly means biannually or biennially.

Examples: The group has biannual meetings. (Two meetings
a year.)
The board members are selected biennially.
(Every two years.)
The group has bimonthly meetings. (Two meetings
a month or one meeting every two months.)
The group has biweekly meetings. (Two meetings
a week or one meeting every two weeks.)
The group has biyearly meetings. (Two meetings
a year or one meeting every two years.)
(To avoid the possibility of confusion, use *twice
yearly, every second year, twice monthly, every
two months, twice weekly,* and *every two
weeks.*)

Bibliography is a list of publications.

Biography is the story of a person's life.

Examples: In the bibliography of your report list books before
             magazines.
             His biography was published in <u>Harper's</u>.

Biennial — See *Biannual*.
Biography — See *Bibliography*.
Birth — See *Berth*.
Bloc is a group with a common interest.
  Block is a piece of wood or an obstacle.

Examples: Our legislators voted as a bloc.
             A piece of metal was imbedded in the wooden
             block.

Born is the past participle of *bear* when used in the passive voice in
the sense of giving birth, except when followed by *by*.
Borne is the past participle of *bear* and means endure. In the
passive voice, if followed by *by*, it may be used in the sense of
giving birth.

Examples: Jim was born on February 28.
             The prince was borne by the queen.
             The crippled man has borne a heavy burden.

Both — See *All*.
Bough — See *Bow*.
Boughten should not be used for *bought*. *Boughten* is strictly dia-
lectic.

Example: This is a bought suit. That one is homemade.

Bouillon is a clear soup.
  Bullion is uncoined silver or gold.

Examples: Max had only a dish of bouillon for lunch.
             Have you ever seen the bullion at Fort Knox?

Bow means to yield.
  Beau is a lover.
  Bough is a tree branch.

Examples: They were forced to bow to the authority.
             Larry is Sally's beau.
             The storm broke several boughs from the elm tree.

Brake means to stop or to slow motion.
  Break means to burst.

Examples: Did he apply the brakes before the wreck?
             Did he brake the car as he started down the hill?

How did he break the window?

Breath is a noun.
  Breathe is a verb.

> Examples: He sat down to catch his breath.
>   Breathe the fresh air.

Bullion — See *Bouillon.*
Bunch should be used only for objects that grow together or are fastened together.

> Example: She bought a bunch of carrots.

Burst is the past tense of *burst. Bursted, bust,* and *busted* are not considered good usage.
But also — See *Not only.*
Buy is a verb.
  By is a preposition.

> Examples: Did you buy supplies today?
>   We passed by your factory.

Calculate and *reckon* should not be used for *suppose.*

> Example: I suppose (not *calculate* or *reckon*) the job will
>   take many weeks.

Calendar is a list of days, weeks, and months arranged in a systematic order.
  Calender means to press into sheets.
  Colander is a cooking utensil.

> Examples: Mark that date on your calendar.
>   That material is ready to be calendered.
>   Put the strawberries in the colander to wash them.

Call — See *Contact.*
Callous means hardened or not sympathetic.
  Callus is hardened skin.

> Examples: He was calloused to such treatment.
>   The callus on his hand was caused by working on
>   the railroad gang.

Can expresses the physical ability of a person to do a thing.
  May shows permission or possibility.

> Examples: Can you lift that weight?
>   May I meet you at your office?

Cannon is a big gun.

Canon is a clergyman or a rule.
Canyon is a deep valley.

Examples: The cannon was placed in the park.
             The canon decreed what could be done.
             The view from the top of the canyon was
                magnificent.

Can't should not be followed by *hardly* or *scarcely* as these combinations form contradictions.

Examples: He can't do that work.
             He can hardly do that work.

Canvas is a cloth used for tents, sails, etc.
Canvass means to solicit or to seek orders, votes, etc.

Examples: He spread a canvas on the floor before he began to
                paint.
             He canvassed the homes in the city before the
                election.

Canyon — See *Cannon.*
Capital is either a noun or an adjective. When it is a noun, it means
the capital city of a state or a stock of accumulated wealth.
Capitol is a noun correctly used only for the building in which a
legislative body meets.

Examples: He invested a great deal of capital in the firm.
             Sacramento is the capital of California.
             Begin every sentence with a capital letter.
             The governor's office is in the capitol.

Carton is a container.
Cartoon is a comical drawing.

Examples: How many cartons of milk did you order?
             He always reads the cartoons in the Sunday paper.

Casual means informal.
Causal refers to a cause.

Examples: That attire is too casual to wear in the office.
             The explanation included the causal factors.

Ceiling is the overhead section of a room.
Sealing is marking with a stamp or securing material in a container.

Examples: What paper did you select for the ceiling?
             The secretaries are sealing all envelopes before
                mailing them.

Censer is an incense burner.
   Censor means to look for objectionable material.
   Censure means to reprimand.
   Census is a count of population.
   Senses are faculties such as seeing, hearing, tasting, feeling, and smelling.

      Examples: Did you see the censer used in the initiation service?
                  All letters the soldier wrote were censored.
                  The official will censure the employee for his actions.
                  A census of the city is taken every ten years.
                  Because of the accident, his senses were impaired.

Cent is one hundredth of a dollar.
   Scent is an odor.
   Sent is the past tense of *send.*

      Examples: They would not pay one cent more than that for the equipment.
                  The scent of burning wood filled the air.
                  The payment was sent before it was due.

Cereal is grain.
   Serial means an arrangement in an order of rank or a continued story.

      Examples: What kind of cereal did you have for breakfast?
                  He is reading a serial in that magazine.

Cession is a withdrawal.
   Session is a meeting.

      Examples: How can you explain the cession of the troops?
                  The board of directors had a long session this morning.

Character is what a person is.
   Reputation is what a person is thought to be.

      Examples: Her character is never questionable.
                  The employee's reputation does not measure up to your requirements.

Choir is a group of singers.
   Quire is 1/20th of a ream.

      Examples: Fifty people sang in the choir.
                  Order three quires of stencils.

Cite is a verb meaning to quote or to draw attention to something.
Sight refers to vision.
Site is a noun which refers to a spot or a location.

> Examples: Cite a passage from one of his writings.
> As we turn the corner, the building will come into sight.
> Bill bought that site for his house.

Client is an individual who employs a professional person, such as a lawyer.
Customer is a person who buys goods.
Patient is one who is treated by a doctor or a dentist.
Patron is a supporter, an advocate, or a defender of an idea.

> Examples: Customers of Bell's Music Store are patrons of the arts.
> The lawyer is a patient of the doctor, but the doctor is a client of the lawyer.

Close, as an adjective, means near or, as a verb, means to shut.
Clothes are garments.

> Examples: His office is close to yours.
> Please close the door.
> Her clothes are of the latest fashions.

Cloth is a noun.
Clothe is a verb.

> Examples: What color is the cloth you bought for the office draperies?
> She will clothe the child in pink tomorrow.

Clothes — See *Close*.
Coarse means rough or inferior in quality.
Course means route.

> Examples: He dumped a load of coarse sand in the parking lot.
> The committee chose its course and proceeded.

Colander — See *Calendar*.
Collision is a clash.
Collusion is a plot or a secret agreement.

> Examples: His car was in a collision last week.
> The dictator was overthrown by the collusion of his cohorts.

Colonel is a military officer.
Kernel is the soft part of a nut or a seed of a cereal.

Examples: The colonel ordered his men to report at dawn.
Chop the pecan kernels for the cake.

Coma is unconsciousness.
Comma is a punctuation mark.

Examples: The injured man is in a coma.
Place a comma between the city and the state.

Command is an order.
Commend is to praise.

Examples: Everyone heard the officer's command.
We will commend him for his good work.

Company — See *Outfit*.
Complacent means satisfied.
Complaisant means desiring to please.

Examples: His complacent attitude will get him nowhere.
In this matter Tom was complaisant.

Complected is not a word of good usage. Use *complectioned*.

Example: She was dark complectioned.

Complement and *compliment* are both nouns and verbs.
Complement means something to make a thing complete or to supply a lack.
Compliment means an expression of admiration or approbation.

Examples: Our office has a complement of five secretaries.
The picture will complement the room.
He should compliment Miss Smith on her
outstanding work.
He gave Miss Smith a compliment.

Compose means to create or to make up the whole.
Comprise means to include. The whole comprises the parts but not vice versa.
Constitute means to make up.

Examples: He has composed many classical numbers.
His territory comprises five states.
The five states constitute his territory.

Condition refers to the quality or the soundness of a person or a thing.
Shape refers to the form or the physical outline of a person or a thing.

Examples: He is in good physical condition (not *shape*).

> Although the tree has a beautiful shape, its
> condition is poor.

Confess is stronger than *admit*.

>   Examples: The thief confessed that he stole the picture.
>   The manager admitted that he made a mistake
>   in the order.

Confidant is a man trusted with secrets.
  Confidante is a woman trusted with secrets.
  Confidence means faith.
  Confident means certain.

>   Examples: Joe is often Melvin's confidant.
>   Joan is often Helen's confidante.
>   We have confidence in his doing excellent work.
>   Are you confident that your answer is correct?

Confidentially means confiding willingly.
  Confidently refers to acting with confidence.

>   Examples: He handled the important matter confidentially.
>   He performed the task confidently.

Congenial means harmonious or compatible.
  Genial means friendly or pleasant.

>   Examples: Everyone in the office is congenial.
>   He has a genial disposition.

Conscience refers to one's feelings of goodness.
  Conscious means aware.

>   Examples: Her conscience was her guide.
>   She was conscious of some of her weaknesses.

Considerable should not be used for *much*.

>   Example: We took much (not *considerable*) time to do the
>   job.

Constitute — See *Compose*.
Consul is a governmental official.
  Council is a noun meaning a body of people assembled for con-
  sultation.
  Counsel is a noun or a verb and means advice or to give advice.

>   Examples: What country does the consul represent?
>   The council met often.
>   The adviser counseled the students.

Contact should not be used for *call* or *write*. It means to touch physically and does not mean to write, call, or telegraph.

> Examples: Please call me at your convenience.
> Please write me when you have questions.

Contemptible means unworthy.
Contemptuous means expressing contempt.

> Examples: She is the most contemptible member of the group.
> She spoke contemptuously of the official.

Continual and *continually* means endless, frequently, or constantly repeated.
Continuous and *continuously* mean without interruption or unbroken.

> Examples: The instructor was interrupted by continual questions.
> Continual delays were the cause of the plant's closing.
> Continuous operation of machinery got the work done.
> The telephone rang continually all day.
> The radio ran continuously from 7 a.m. to 10 p.m.

Convicted means found guilty.
Convinced means proved.

> Examples: He was convicted of manslaughter.
> The saleman convinced us that we should buy the machine.

Copy is a transcript of an original work.
Facsimile is a reproduction of an item.
Replica is a reproduction by the original artist of a statue or a picture.

> Examples: Type a copy of this letter.
> Draw a facsimile of the design.
> The replica was placed in the hallway.

Core is the central part.
Corps is a group of people.

> Examples: The core of the apple was rotten.
> His special theory was the core of his argument.
> A corps of engineers took charge of the work.

Costume means wearing apparel.
Custom is usual practice.

Examples: Describe the costume she wore to the party.
             Custom dictates that you dress as others do.

Could implies ability.
   Might means may and implies probability or permission.
   Mite is a small creature found on plants, animals, and fowls.

Examples: Could he lift the machine?
             The mail might be late today.
             The bird was covered with mites.

Council — See *Consul.*
Counsel — See *Consul.*
Couple refers to a pair and should not be used for *two.*

Examples: He will leave in two (not *a couple of*) hours.
             The party was for couples only.

Course — See *Coarse.*
Creak means to squeak.
   Creek is a stream of water.

Examples: The stairs creak.
             Heavy rains caused the creek to overflow.

Credible means believable.
   Creditable means with credit.
   Credulous means believing too easily.

Examples: He gave a credible report.
             He has a creditable reputation as a salesman.
             She is usually too credulous to joke.

Creek — See *Creak.*
Criteria — See *Data.*
Critic is a person who evaluates something.
   Critique is a criticism.

Examples: Professor Langworthy is to be a critic of the
                performance.
             Mr. Lawson wrote a critique of the play.

Currant is a small fruit.
   Current is a movement of water or electricity.

Examples: Currant jelly is on the table.
             Electric current was soon restored after the storm.

Custom — See *Costume.*
Customer — See *Client.*
Cymbal is a brass musical plate.
   Symbol is a sign.

Examples: The cymbals crashed at the close of the
composition.
What symbol represents that organization?

Damage applies only to property.
Injury is impairment of something and applies to reputations,
character, and persons.

Examples: How much damage did the hail do to the roof?
His injuries were the result of an automobile
accident.

Data, memoranda, phenomena, criteria, and *strata* are plural and are
used with plural verbs. Through common misuse, *data* is becoming acceptable as a singular noun.

Example: The data you need have been received.

Decease means die.
Disease is sickness.

Example: The will of the deceased was read.
Many diseases are not contagious.

Decent means adequate.
Descent means the going from higher to lower positions.
Dissent means to disagree.

Examples: We haven't had a decent rain this month.
The elevator stuck on its descent from the tenth
floor to the lobby.
The bill was passed by the legislature without
dissent.

Decree is a court decision or an order.
Degree is a measure of temperature or a college title conferred
when a course of study is completed.

Examples: Rulers decreed that taxes must be increased.
Mr. Swenson completed a graduate degree this
spring.
How many degrees did the maximum
temperature vary this week?

Deduce means to draw a conclusion.
Deduct means subtract.

Examples: What did you deduce from the lecture?
Deduct 10 percent from the amount due.

Deduction means from the whole to the parts or from the general to
the specific.

Induction means from the parts to the whole or from the specific to the general.

> Examples: After observing the group, we concluded through deduction that its members were fanatics.
> After observing the members, we concluded through induction that the group was unstable.

Defer means to postpone.
  Deter means to inhibit.
  Differ means to vary.

> Examples: Payment will be deferred until you receive your check.
> The change in policy will not deter our progress.
> How does your product differ from ours?

Deference means respect for other people.
  Difference means distinction.

> Examples: He performed that act out of deference to Mr. Nelson.
> What is the difference in quality in these materials?

Degree — See *Decree*.
Delusion — See *Allusion*.
Dependence means reliance.
  Dependents are people who rely on others for financial support.

> Examples: He places much dependence on Mr. Riley's suggestions.
> How many dependents can he claim for income-tax purposes?

Depositary is a person trusted with things.
  Depository is a place where things are deposited.

> Examples: Mr. Simpson asked Mr. Birch to act as his depositary.
> The group uses the Shawnee Bank as its depository.

Deposition is written testimony.
  Disposition is attitude toward people and things.

> Examples: The lawyer took a deposition from Mr. Jones, who was ill and unable to attend the trial.
> His disposition is usually pleasant.

Depository — See *Depositary*.
Deprecate means to disapprove.
  Depreciate means to decrease in value.

Examples: He deprecated the action taken by the group.
            A new car depreciates rapidly.

Descent — See *Decent.*
  Desert, as a noun, is an arid piece of land. As a verb, *desert* means
  to abandon.
  Dessert is the last course of a meal.

Examples: Irrigation is used on the desert.
            Only after sinking was imminent, did the crew
              desert the ship.
            We had pie for dessert.

Desolate means forsaken or barren.
  Dissolute means lacking restraint.

Examples: Did you ever see so much desolate country?
            His conduct was dissolute.

Dessert — See *Desert.*
Deter — See *Defer.*
Detract means to take away from.
  Distract means to confuse or divert.

Examples: The dirty windows will detract from the
              appearance of the office.
            The noise during the lecture will distract the
              audience.

Device is a mechanism.
  Devise means to invent.

Examples: What devices were used to accomplish your
              purposes?
            They devised many schemes to be considered.

Dice are cubes used in games.
  Dies means passes from life.
  Dyes means colorings or stains.

Examples: The dice were loaded.
            When he dies, he will leave a large estate.
            We had several brown dyes from which to choose.

Differ — See *Defer.*
Difference — See *Deference.*
Different should be followed by *from*, not *than*.

Example: This ream of paper is different from that ream.

Different may be superfluous as an adjective in many situations.

Example: Ten (not *ten different*) classifications were made.

Dining means eating.
   Dinning is a verb, a noun, or an adjective and means a loud noise.

   Examples: We are dining at the club tomorrow.
               The dinning of the bell disturbed the audience.

Disapprove means to object or not to approve.
   Disprove means to prove that something is not true.

   Examples: The plans for the building were disapproved.
               That theory has been disproved.

Disburse means to pay.
   Dispense means to distribute, to exempt, or to do without.
   Disperse means to dispel.

   Examples: How much was disbursed for the housing?
               Can't we dispense with such activities?
               The officers will disperse the crowd.

Disease — See *Decease.*
Disinterested means lacking interest or being impartial.
   Uninterested means not having the mind engaged or not interested.

   Examples: He is a disinterested person.
               She is uninterested in what is being said.

Disorganized means that organization does not exist where it former-
   ly existed.
   Unorganized means that organization has never existed.

   Examples: The club became disorganized after several
                   members moved away.
               The unorganized group protested the decision.

Dispense — See *Disburse.*
Disperse — See *Disburse.*
Disposition — See *Deposition.*
Disprove — See *Disapprove.*
Disremember is colloquial and is not considered good usage.
Dissent — See *Decent.*
Dissolute — See *Desolate.*
Distract — See *Detract.*
Divers — See *Adverse.*
Diverse — See *Adverse.*
Doesn't is a contraction of *does not.*
   Don't is a contraction of *do not.*

   Examples: He doesn't type very well.

It doesn't matter which typewriter is used.
They don't like his music.

Dragged is the past tense of *drag*.
Drug refers to medicine.

Examples: They dragged the boxes into the storeroom.
They drugged the madman to subdue him.
The doctor prescribed a powerful drug for him.

Dual refers to two.
Duel is a combat between two persons.

Examples: His dual responsibilities became burdensome.
The knights fought a duel.

Due to modifies nouns and pronouns.
Because of modifies verbs and adverbs.

Examples: Her resignation was due to illness.
She resigned because of illness.

Duel — See *Dual*.
Dyeing means coloring with dye.
Dying means passing from life.

Examples: She is dyeing the draperies brown.
Many people are dying on holidays.

Dyes — See *Dice*.
Each other is used to refer to two things or two persons.
One another is used to refer to more than two things or persons.

Examples: The two brothers looked like each other.
The members of the ball team congratulated one
another at the end of the game.

Eager — See *Anxious*.
Easier is an adjective used in comparing two things.
More easily is an adverb used in comparing two things.

Examples: For her, typewriting is easier than shorthand.
She learned typewriting more easily than
shorthand.

Economic refers to economics.
Economical means thrifty.

Examples: We gathered economic data from the Bureau of the
Census.
The machine is economical to operate.

Effect — See *Affect*.
Elicit means to bring out.
   Illicit means not lawful.

      Examples: His questions elicited many responses.
                    His acts were illicit.

Elusive means evasive.
   Illusive means deceptive.

      Examples: He had some elusive qualities.
                    His illusive planning was detected.

Emanate means to come out.
   Emulate means to imitate.

      Examples: Water emanated from the side of the hill.
                    The young assistant tried to emulate his boss.

Emerge means to come out.
   Immerge is an intransitive verb and means to dip into.
   Immerse is a transitive verb and means to dip into.

      Examples: The car emerged from the fog.
                    They immerged into the water.
                    They immersed themselves in water.

Emigrants go out of a country. (*E* for *exit*)
   Immigrants come into a country. (*I* for *into*)

      Examples: He is an emigrant from Spain.
                    He is an immigrant in America.

      (Note: *Inmigration* and *outmigration* are becoming popular substitutes for *immigration* and *emigration*, respectively.)

Eminent means distinguished.
   Imminent means threatening.

      Examples: The speaker was an eminent statesman.
                    A bad storm is imminent.

Emulate — See *Emanate*.
Endorse — See *Approve*.
Enthuse is a colloquial word and is not considered good usage.
   Enthusiastic is the correct word.

      Examples: I am enthusiastic (not *enthused*) about my new job.

Envelop is a verb.
   Envelope is a noun.

      Examples: Smoke soon will envelop the barn.
                    Put a stamp on the envelope.

Equable means uniform.
   Equitable means fair or just.

      Examples: He was known for his equable handling of
                  matters.
                  He made an equitable distribution of the profits.

Equally and *as* should not be used together.

      Examples: The two men seem equally (not *equally as*) alert.
                  Mr. Brand manages as well as (not *equally as well
                  as*) Mr. Forbes.

Equally is often misspelled *equaly*.
Equally should not be used instead of *just*.

      Example: In ten years your car will run just as well as it
                 does now.

Equitable — See *Equable*.
Erasable means that something can be erased.
   Irascible means easily angered.

      Examples: That typographical error is erasable.
                  Both brothers are irascible.

Ere means before.
   Err means to make a mistake.

      Examples: Do that ere dawn.
                  Frank erred in signing the contract.

Eruption is a breaking out.
   Irruption means rushing in.

      Examples: The political unrest caused an eruption of border
                  clashes.
                  There was an irruption of water into homes after
                  the dike broke.

Etc. — See *And*.
Even — See *Only*.
Every day is a noun modified by an adjective.
   Everyday is an adjective.

      Examples: The serviceman visits the office every day.
                  This is an everyday occurrence.

Every one points out a distinct person or thing.
   Everyone means that all are included.

      Examples: Every one of the employees received a salary
                  increase.

Everyone should study his lesson.

Everyday — See *Every day.*
Everyone — See *Every one.*
Everywheres is incorrectly used for *everywhere.*
Exceed — See *Accede.*
Except — See *Accept.*
Excess — See *Access.*
Excuse connotes apology.
   Reason is cause for an action and does not connote apology.

   Example: He gave many excuses for his absences but no
                    good reasons.

Excuse is in better usage socially than *pardon.*
Expand means enlarge.
   Expend means to pay out or to use up.

   Examples: How soon can the facilities be expanded?
                    The company expended more money than it
                    took in.

Expansive means large.
   Expensive means costly.

   Examples: The halls in the mansion were expansive.
                    The paper you used is very expensive.

Expatiate means to write or speak for a long time or to wander.
   Expiate means to pay a penalty.

   Examples: The professor expatiated during his lecture.
                    The culprit will expiate his misdeeds.

Expect — See *Anticipate.*
Expend — See *Expand.*
Expensive — See *Expansive.*
Expiate — See *Expatiate.*
Explicit means distinct.
   Implicit means implied.

   Examples: Explicit instructions were given for the project.
                    Was there anything implicit in his remark?

Extant means existing.
   Extent means distance or range.
   Extinct means not existing.

   Examples: That species is extant.
                    To what extent did he go to achieve his purpose?
                    Dinosaurs are extinct.

Extra is not correctly used for *unusually* or *very*.

> Examples: The cast gave an unusually (not *extra*) good
> performance.
> He was very glad to receive the message.

Facetious means humorous or witty.
  Fictitious means imaginary.

> Examples: He made a facetious remark.
> The report was mostly fictitious.

Facsimile — See *Copy*.
Faint means weak.
  Feint means pretense.

> Examples: She felt faint.
> That maneuver was a feint.

Fair means impartial or just.
  Fare is the price paid for transportation.

> Examples: Do his employees receive fair treatment?
> Train fares have been reduced recently.

Farther refers to distance.
  Further refers to extent or amount.

> Examples: Gary traveled farther than Leon.
> Send me further information.
> We shall study the problem further.

Fate is destiny.
  Fete means an elaborate party or to honor.

> Examples: Have you heard the fate of the three men?
> How many attended the fete at the president's
> home?

Faze means to disturb composure.
  Phase means a part of a cycle or an aspect.

> Examples: The irrelevant remarks will not faze him.
> The second phase of the program begins next week.

Feat is a deed.
  Feet is the plural of *foot*.

> *Examples:*   The acrobats performed an unusual feat.
> How many feet did he fall?

Fee refers to a price paid for professional services.

Salary refers to remuneration for services rendered during a period of time.

Wage refers to remuneration paid according to hours worked or units produced.

    Examples: The lawyer's fee was $1,000 for handling the case.
                   The secretary received a salary of $500 a month.
                   The ditchdigger received a wage of $2 an hour.

Feet — See *Feat.*
Feint — See *Faint.*
Fete — See *Fate.*
Fewer refers to number.
  Less denotes quantity.

    Examples: Fewer people were hired this year than last year.
                   He drank less coffee today than yesterday.
                   He drank fewer cups of coffee today than
                   yesterday.

Fiancé refers to a man engaged to be married.
  Fiancée refers to a woman engaged to be married.

    Examples: George is Mary's fiancé.
                   Mary is George's fiancée.

Fictitious — See *Facetious.*
Figuratively means represented symbolically.
  Literally means reproduced word for word or adhering to the facts.

    Examples: He interpreted the passage figuratively.
                   He translated the poem literally.

Figure should not be used for the noun *price* or the verb *suppose.*

    Examples: The price (not *figure*) quoted on the house is too
                   high.
                   I suppose (not *figure*) the time is right for
                   investing in the stock.

Finally means at last.
  Finely is the adverbial form of *fine.*

    Examples: We finally arrived at our destination.
                   The ingredients were finely ground.

Fine should not be used for *well.*

    Example: He works well (not *fine*) with the men.

Finely — See *Finally.*
Finished — See *Through* listed under *Thorough.*

Firm — See *Outfit.*

First-rate is an adjective and should not be used as an adverb.

>   Example: He did a first-rate job. (Not: He handled the job
>   first-rate.)

Fiscal means financial.
>   *Physical* refers to material items.

>   Examples: Those reports should be made at the end of the
>   fiscal year.
>   His physical condition is excellent.

Flaunt means to make a boastful display.
>   *Flout* means to scorn or to scoff.

>   Examples: The salesman flaunts his recent promotion.
>   The committee flouted the assistant's suggestion.

Flew is the past tense of *fly.*
>   *Flu* is an illness.
>   *Flue* is a chimney.

>   Examples: Those birds flew high above the trees.
>   Half of the office staff was absent because of the
>   flu.
>   The flue carried out the gas fumes.

Flounder means to struggle or to move awkwardly.
>   *Founder* means to become disabled or to sink.

>   Examples: The committee floundered about with divergent
>   opinions.
>   The horse will founder from overeating.
>   The ship foundered at sea.

Flout — See *Flaunt.*
Flu — See *Flew.*
Flue — See *Flew.*
Formally means in a formal manner.
>   *Formerly* means previously.

>   Examples: Jean dressed formally for the party.
>   Mr. Simmons formerly taught mathematics.

Former specifies the first of two people or things named.
>   *Latter* specifies the second of two people or things named.

>   Examples: The former machine was bought in 1950.
>   The latter machine was bought in 1964.

Forth means onward.

Fourth refers to four; *forty* is not spelled with a *u*.

Examples: They went forth to overcome obstacles.
                      Sally works at the fourth desk on the west side.

Fortuitous means to occur by chance or by accident and is not a good synonym for *fortunate*.
Fortunate means good or lucky.

Example: We were fortunate to be able to take advantage of the fortuitous situation.

Foul means offensive.
   Fowl is a bird.

Examples: The foul odor is coming from an industry nearby.
                      Chicken is the only fowl to be served at the banquet.

Founder — See *Flounder*.
Fourth — See *Forth*.
Fowl — See *Foul*.
Freeze means to make into ice.
   Frieze means coarse wool.

Examples: When the lakes freeze, we may skate.
                      The divan upholstery is frieze.

Funny means humorous and should never be used for *strange* or *odd*.

Example: His sudden departure was strange (not *funny*).

Further — See *Farther*.
Gamble means to speculate.
   Gambol means to jump in playing.

Examples: They gambled on the outcome of the game.
                      The lambs gamboled in the pasture.

Gap means an opening.
   Gape means to yawn or to stare.

Examples: The construction men left a gap in the center of the wall.
                      He gaped during the lecture.

Generally refers to overall and not to specific incidents.
   Usually refers to normal occurrence of events.

Examples: Generally speaking, the employees will be pleased with the change of policy.
                      Usually the treasurer objects to changes in policy.

Genial — See *Congenial.*

Gentleman and *lady* connote refinement.

  Man and *woman* make no distinction of refinement.

> Examples: He is only a man until he proves himself to be a
>   gentleman.
>   She is only a woman until she proves herself to be
>   a lady.

(Note: In addressing groups, give the audience the benefit of
doubt and say, "Ladies and Gentlemen.")

Gilt means gold.

  Guilt means misconduct.

> Examples: The plate has a gilt edge.
>   Finally he confessed his guilt.

Gist means main idea.

  Jest means joke.

  Just means only or fair.

> Examples: Give us in one sentence the gist of the matter.
>   He made the remark in jest.
>   He made just a passing mark on the examination.

Good, an adjective, should not be used for *well*, an adverb.

> Example: He read well (not *good*).

Use adjectives to describe verbs that refer to the five senses, e.g.,
taste, feel, look, sound, and *smell.*

> Correct: She feels bad.
>   He looks good.
>   That coffee smells good.
>   That music sounds good.
>   The pie tastes good.
>   The cake tastes terrible.

> Incorrect: She feels well.
>   He looks well.

When referring to someone's state of health, use these expressions:
> She feels as if she is well.
> She feels well (as opposed to feeling ill).
> He looks as if he is well.

Grate means a frame made of bars.

  Great means large.

> Examples: Clean the grate of the fireplace.
>   That organization does a great deal of good.

Greatly appreciate is incorrect because, by definition, *appreciate* implies great or heightened perception.

    Example: He appreciated (not *greatly appreciated*) all you did for him.

Guarantee is a verb.
  Guaranty is a noun.

    Examples: The company will guarantee the tires for 12,000 miles.
                 He placed his guaranty in the glove compartment.

Guessed is the past tense of *guess.*
  Guest is a visitor.

    Examples: The secretary guessed the weight of the package.
                 We shall have two guests in the office tomorrow.

Guilt — See *Gilt.*
Hanged is properly used as the past tense of *hang* when referring to putting to death.

    Examples: He was hanged (not *hung*) by the neck until dead.
                 He hanged himself in the garage.
                 The football coach was hanged in effigy.
                 He hung the picture on the wall.

Heal means to cure.
  Heel is part of the foot.

    Examples: The wound healed slowly.
                 His new shoe rubbed a blister on his heel.

Healthful is an adjective meaning contributing to good health.
  Healthy applies to a person in good health.

    Examples: Fruit is a healthful food.
                 John is a healthy boy.

Hear means to get information through the ears.
  Here means in this place.

    Examples: Can you hear what he is saying?
                 Place the supplies here in the top drawer of the desk.

Hearsay is something heard from other people.
  Heresy is an idea contrary to accepted beliefs.

    Examples: That report is based on hearsay and not on facts.
                 His actions were interpreted as heresy.

Heel — See *Heal.*
Here — See *Hear.*
Heresy — See *Hearsay.*
Herself, himself, myself, and yourself (See *self* under "Pronouns" in "Grammar Problems," p. 65.)
Hew means to chop or to carve.
   Hue means color.

      Examples: The monument was hewed of granite.
                  The hue in that material is vivid.

Higher is the comparative degree of *high.*
   Hire means employ.

      Examples: He received a higher salary this year than last year.
                  Whom did you hire for the sales position?

Himself — See *Herself.*
Hoard means to hide a supply.
   Horde means a group of people.

      Examples: The eccentric man hoarded his money.
                  The horde descended on the village at night.

Hoarse means raspy.
   Horse is an animal.

      Examples: Because of a cold, his voice was hoarse.
                  He rode the horse in the parade.

Hole is an opening.
   Whole means entire.

      Examples: A hole was drilled in the wall.
                  The whole project is difficult.

Holey refers to holes.
   Holly is a shrub or the foliage of a shrub.
   Holy means sacred.
   Wholly means entirely.

      Examples: The sweater was holey.
                  Decorate the room with holly.
                  The holy cross was easily seen.
                  The explanation was wholly satisfactory.

Horde — See *Hoard.*
Horse — See *Hoarse.*
Hue — See *Hew.*
Human, an adjective, which should not be used as a noun, refers to the characteristics of mankind.

Humane means sympathetic or considerate.

Examples: He is a human being. (Not: He is a *human*.)
His reactions were human.
He works for a humane society.

Hypercritical means overly critical.
Hypocritical means assuming good qualities not possessed.

Examples: He was hypercritical of the results.
He often assumes a hypocritical attitude.

If and *whether* are conjunctions. Use *whether* after the words *see*, *know*, *learn*, and *doubt*. Use *if* to begin clauses expressing a condition.

Examples: Let me know whether (not *if*) you can go.
He will go if his brother goes.

Illicit — See *Elicit.*
Illusion — See *Allusion.*
Illusive — See *Elusive.*
Imitate means to copy.
Intimate means familiar, close, or to hint.

Examples: The child imitated the actions of his father.
They are intimate friends.
What did Frank intimate that we should do?

Immerge — See *Emerge.*
Immerse — See *Emerge.*
Immigrants — See *Emigrants.*
Imminent — See *Eminent.*
Immunity means resistance to a certain disease.
Impunity means freedom from punishment.

Examples: During a period of ten years he built up immunities to many diseases.
Two members of the group gained impunity.

Implicit — See *Explicit.*
Imply means suggest.
Infer means to draw a conclusion.

Examples: She implied that I made an error.
He inferred from the letter that Paul was ill.

In indicates that a person or a thing is inside an enclosure. (Position)
Into means going from the outside to the inside. (Direction)

Examples: The manager is in his office.

The assistants went from the street into the building.

Inane means lacking significance or relevance.
   Insane means not sane.

   Examples: The whole idea is inane.
              His partner became insane this past year.

Incidence is an occurrence.
   Incidents are concomitant events subordinate to other events or actions likely to lead to grave consequences.

   Examples: In this incidence we will take the second alternative.
              Snubbing foreign diplomats creates incidents that may cause breaks in diplomatic relations.

Incidentally is commonly misspelled *incidently*.
Incidents — See *Incidence*.
Incinerate means to burn.
   Insinuate means to imply.

   Examples: He has taken the trash to the burner to incinerate it.
              What was he insinuating when he made that remark?

Incite means to stir up.
   Insight means discernment.

   Examples: The speaker incited the audience to take action.
              His insight into the problem was amazing.

Incredible means unbelievable.
   Incredulous means unbelieving.

   Examples: He gave an incredible report of the accident.
              The audience was incredulous.

Indict means to accuse or to charge.
   Indite is to put in writing.

   Examples: The grand jury will indict him early this week.
              The scribe can indite a great deal of material in a short time.

Individual — See *Persons*.
Induction — See *Deduction*.
Infamous refers to infamy or disgrace.
   Noted means renowned.

Notorious gives a negative connotation and means famous.

> Examples: December 7, 1941, was an infamous day in history.
> Einstein was a noted physicist.
> Jesse James was a notorious outlaw.

Infer — See *Imply.*
Informed should be used instead of *posted.*
   Post means to place in a location, as on a wall.
   Posted, meaning informed, is colloquial and is not considered good usage. (See *Posted.*)

> Examples: Mr. Nelson is one of the best-informed men in his field.
> The notice was posted on the bulletin board.

Ingenious means original or marked with intelligence.
   Ingenuous means straightforward or innate.

> Examples: His inventions demonstrate his ingenious mind.
> He certainly was ingenuous in his remarks.

Injury — See *Damage.*
Insane — See *Inane.*
Insight — See *Incite.*
Insinuate — See *Incinerate.*
Insoluble means not dissolvable.
   Insolvable means not solvable.
   Insolvent means having more liabilities than assets.

> Examples: This powder is insoluble.
> This problem is insolvable.
> His business is insolvent.

Instance is an event.
   Instants are small amounts of time.

> Examples: In this instance he could not prove his point.
> He will be here in a few instants.

Intellectual refers to a mind used in acquiring education and seeking culture.
   Intelligent refers to a mind that is alert and capable of solving problems.

> Examples: He is engaged in many intellectual pursuits.
> He is intelligent enough that he should do well in that subject.

Intend — See *Aim.*
Intense means very large or great.

Intents means purposes.

> Examples: The heat was intense.
> This is practical for all intents.

Intermural means between walls, cities, or colleges.
Intramural means within the walls, the city, or the college.

> Examples: An intermural game was played between the
> University of Kansas and the University of
> Oklahoma.
> The fraternities played an intramural game.

Interstate means between states.
Intrastate means within a state.

> Examples: That interstate shipment was from California to
> Oregon.
> You must pay Kansas sales tax on an intrastate
> shipment.

Intimate — See *Imitate*.
Into — See *In*.
Intolerable means unbearable.
Intolerant means not willing to consider the viewpoints of others.

> Examples: The heat this week has been almost intolerable.
> Some religious groups are intolerant of the beliefs
> of other groups.

Intramural — See *Intermural*.
Intrastate — See *Interstate*.
Inverse — See *Adverse*.
Invite should not be used for *invitation*.

> Example: We received an invitation (not *an invite*) to the
> open house.

Irascible — See *Erasable*.
Irregardless is not considered to be in good usage. Use *regardless*.
Irritate — See *Aggravate*.
Irruption — See *Eruption*.
Its is a possessive pronoun.
It's is a contraction of *it is*.

> Examples: The company raised its prices.
> It's a difficult task to perform.

Jest — See *Gist*.
Just — See *Only* and *Gist*.
Kernel — See *Colonel*.

Key is a device for locking and unlocking doors.
  Quay is a landing place for ships.

  Examples: Have another key made for the office door.
              That ship is being unloaded at the quay.

Kind is singular; so singular words, such as *this* and *that*, are used
  before it.

  Examples: Try this kind of ink.
              Try these kinds of inks.

Kind of and *sort of* should not be used instead of *rather* or *somewhat*.
  Use *kind of* and *sort of* only when *type* can be substituted for
kind and *sort*.

  Examples: What kind of book is that? (What type of book is
              that?)
              What sort of an arrangement shall we use?
              I should rather like to go.
              I am somewhat interested in the business.

Kindly should not be used instead of *please*.

  Example: Please (not *kindly*) send me your check today.

Knew is the past tense of *know*.
  New means recent.

  Examples: He knew what the answer would be before he
              asked.
              In his lecture he presented many new ideas.

Know should be followed by *that*, not by *as*.

  Example: He does not know that (not know as) he can do
              that work well.

Lady — See *Gentleman*.
Last refers to the final item of several items or a series of items.
  Latest means most recent.
  Past refers to something that has previously taken place.

  Examples: The last two weeks of the four-week program were
              busy ones.
              Your latest order has been received.
              The past two weeks have been cold.

Later specifically relates to the comparison of two things.
  Latter refers to the end.

Examples: Friday is later in the week than Tuesday.
Friday is in the latter part of the week.

Latest — See *Last.*
Latter — See *Former* and *Later.*
Lay — See *Lay,* p. 69.
Lead is a metal or is the present tense of the infinitive *to lead.*
  Led is the past tense of *lead.*

Examples: These men now lead the organizations listed.
He dropped molten lead on his foot.
He led the group discussion.

Lean means lacking fat.
  Lien is a mortgage.

Examples: She eats only lean meat.
The lien was placed on that house in 1962.

Learn signifies the acquisition of knowledge.
  Teach indicates that knowledge is given to some person or thing.

Examples: Spencer learned a lesson quickly.
The supervisor will teach him to operate the new
      machine.

Leased is the past tense of *lease,* meaning to rent with a contract.
  Least means smallest.

Examples: They leased the building for ten years.
That is the least salary he will accept.

Least — See *Less* and *Leased.*
Leave should never be used to mean *let.*

Examples: Let (not *leave*) him do the work.
Let (not *leave*) him be.

Led — See *Lead.*
Legislator is a member of the legislature.
  Legislature is a group making laws.

Examples: The legislator from our district approved of the
      ideas presented.
When will the legislature meet again?

Lend is a verb.
  Loan, a noun meaning something borrowed, is only carelessly used
as a verb.
  Lone means only.

Examples: Will you lend (not *loan*) me your book?

> The loan was approved for their new home.
> He is the lone survivor of the wreck.

Less is used to compare two quantities. (See *Fewer*.)
  Least is used to compare more than two quantities.

Examples: She used less paper today than she did yesterday.
            Today she used the least paper that she has used
            this week.

Lessee is one who leases property from another.
  Lessor is one who leases property to another.
  Lesser is the comparative degree of *less*.

Examples: Mr. Smith, the lessee, leased the new building from
            Mr. Jones, the lessor.
            Which do you consider the lesser of the two evils.

Lessen means to decrease.
  Lesson means instruction for learning.

Examples: Will his work load be lessened this month?
            All of us can learn a lesson from his example.

Lesser — See *Lessee*.
Lesson — See *Lessen*.
Lessor — See *Lessee*.
Let — See *Leave*.
Levee is a bank to hold water.
  Levy means assessment.

Examples: The levee broke during the flood.
            The tax levy has been raised this year.

Liable — See *Apt*.
Libel — See *Apt*.
Lie — See *Lie*, p. 69.
Lien — See *Lean*.
Lightening means that something is made lighter.
  Lightning is an electrical flash of light.

Examples: The company is lightening its work load.
            Much lightning accompanied the storm.

Like is a preposition and must be followed by an object, a noun, or a
pronoun.
  Like is also a verb.
  As if and *as* are conjunctions and are followed by verbal forms,
clauses, and phrases.

Examples: Mary looks like her mother.

This problem is like one we had last week.
I like my work.
She talks as if she knows all the answers.
You do not live as we do.

Likely — See *Apt.*
Likely should not be used for *probably.*

Example: She will probably (not *likely*) come to the office
early today.

Literally — See *Figuratively.*
Load is cargo.
Lode is an ore deposit.

Examples: A load of sand was delivered yesterday.
They found the lode years ago.

Loan — See *Lend.*
Loath means reluctant.
Loathe is a verb meaning to dislike.

Examples: I am loath to discuss that matter now.
Many people loathe such actions.

Local specifies a limited location.
Locale is a place.

Examples: Do you read the local papers?
He described the locale vividly.

Locate should not be used for *settle.*

Example: The pioneers settled (not *located*) in the West.

Lode — See *Load.*
Lone — See *Lend.*
Loose is an adjective.
Lose is a verb.

Examples: The clamp on the machine is loose.
When did you lose your check?

Luxuriant means vigorous or rank growth.
Luxurious pertains to luxury.

Example: The luxuriant plants impressed the visitors at the
open house of the luxurious apartment
building.

Mad — See *Angry.*
Magnate is an influential person.
Magnet is a device that attracts metal.

Examples: Mr. Pearson is a magnate in his industry.
                  Use the magnet to pick up the paper clips.

Magnificent means extremely beautiful.
   Munificent means generous.

Examples: The scenery is magnificent.
                  Mr. Parsons has always been munificent to higher
                  education.

Mailed — See *Posted.*
Main means *principal.*
   Mane is hair growing on an animal's neck.

Examples: The main attraction at the convention was your
                  exhibit.
                  That horse's mane is beautiful.

Majority means more than half of the number.
   Plurality means a larger number of votes than those for any other
   candidate. A plurality need not be a majority, more than half.
   Quorum is a minimum number of members of a group agreed upon
   to conduct business.

Examples: A majority of the members voted for him.
                  A plurality was required to defeat his two
                  opponents.
                  Since a quorum was present, the commission
                  transacted its business.

Mane — See *Main.*
Manner is a way of acting or doing something.
   Manor is a dwelling or an estate.

Examples: Did you like the manner in which he handled the
                  situation?
                  He moved into the manor last month.

Many — See *Much.*
Marital refers to marriage.
   Marshall means to put in order.
   Martial means military.

Examples: The couple consulted the marriage counselor about
                  their marital problems.
                  The forces were marshalled at dawn.
                  The president declared martial law.

Material refers to tangible matter from which things are made.
   Materiel is equipment or supplies used by an organization.

Examples: The material in the suit is silk.
            The ordnance plant has a large supply of materiel.

May — See *Can*.
May be is a verb.
  Maybe means perhaps.

Examples: The package may be delivered today.
            Maybe the package will be delivered today.

Mean means cruel or is an arithmetic average.
  Mien means bearing.

Examples: Mr. Forbes was mean to his secretary.
            The mean temperature for the month was 72
              degrees.
            Harry's mien was favorable during the session.

Meat is animal flesh.
  Meet means to come together.
  Mete means to allot.

Examples: The meat served at the banquet was delicious.
            Can you meet with the committee tomorrow?
            The distributor meted out the available food to its
              dealers.

Memoranda — See *Data*.
Merely — See *Only*.
Mete — See *Meat*.
Mien — See *Mean*.
Might — See *Could*.
Mighty means strong and does not mean very or extremely.

Example: James did very (not *mighty*) well his first day at
            work.

Miner is one who takes ore from the ground.
  Minor is a person not of age.

Examples: Twelve miners were trapped in the coal mine.
            Intoxicating beverages are not be be sold to a
              minor.

Missed is the past tense of *miss*.
  Mist is small particles of moisture.

Examples: Harry missed the bus because he overslept.
            Mist fell during the lunch hour.

Mite — See *Could*.
Monetary relates to money.

Monitory means warning.

> Examples: What monetary consideration is he asking?
>   What monitory duty does the proctor perform?

Moral means conforming to a standard of what is good or bad.
  Morale means the prevailing mood.

> Examples: This problem being considered is a moral one.
>   The morale of the employees is excellent.

Morality refers to moral — good or bad.
  Mortality refers to mortal — life and death.

> Examples: The minister spoke about morality in society.
>   The insurance company revised its mortality
>   tables.

More is used when comparing two persons or things.
  Most, the superlative degree of *many*, is used when comparing more
  than two persons or things.
  Almost means nearly.

> Examples: Mrs. Allen is more efficient than Mrs. Stone.
>   Mrs. Allen filed most of the 50 cards yesterday.
>   Mrs. Allen is the most efficient secretary in the
>   company.
>   Almost half the students went on the tour.

More easily — See *Easier.*
Morning is the time from midnight to noon.
  Mourning is grief because of a death.

> Examples: Did he say what time this morning he will arrive?
>   That nation is mourning the loss of one of its
>   leaders.

Mortality — See *Morality.*
Motif is a design.
  Motive is a desire to act.

> Examples: Can you describe the motif he used in his latest
>   work?
>   What motive did he have for doing such a thing?

Mourning — See *Morning.*
Much refers to quantity. (See *Considerable.*)
  Many refers to number.

> Examples: How much money did she spend for supplies?
>   How many dollars were spent for supplies?

Munificent — See *Magnificent.*
Myself — See *Herself.*
Nearly — See *Only* and *Around.*
New — See *Knew.*
No one — See *Any body* and *Any one.*
Not only must be followed by *but also.*

> Example: The company not only raised wages but also
> increased fringe benefits.

Noted — See *Infamous.*
Notorious — See *Infamous.*
Nowheres is incorrectly used for *nowhere.*
Number — See *Amount.*
Occasion is a happening or an incident.
  Opportunity is a condition or a favorable circumstance.

> Examples: The long-awaited occasion is scheduled for July 5.
> On that day I hope to have an opportunity to
> meet you.

Of should never be used for *have* in such expressions as *could have,
should have, would have,* or *may have.*

> Example: He should have (not *of*) gone to the meeting earlier.

On is an adverb or a preposition.
  Onto is a preposition.

> Examples: We went on to the meeting.
> From the house we walked onto the patio.
> He went on to discuss the proposition.

One another — See *Each other.*
Only, just, merely, nearly, and *even* should be placed immediately
before the words they modify.

> Examples: Only Mary could work the first problem. (Nobody
> else)
> Mary could only work the first problem. (But
> could not explain it)
> Mary could work only the first problem. (Could
> not do the other problems)
> Just Mary could work the first problem.
> Mary could just work the first problem.
> Mary could work just the first problem.

Onto — See *On.*
Opaque describes an object that cannot be seen through.
  Transparent describes an object that can be seen through.

Examples: To block out the light, use an opaque paint for
            coating the glass.
            They replaced the glass with transparent plastic.

Opportunity — See *Occasion.*
Ordinance is a law, a regulation, or a formal rule.
  Ordnance refers to military supplies or weapons.

Examples: A new ordinance provides for one-way traffic on
            Maine Street.
            That ordnance plant makes explosives.

Ought — See *Aught.*
Out loud should not be used for *aloud.*

Example: The president read the report aloud.

Outfit should not be used for *firm* or *company.*

Example: The firm (not *outfit*) sells furniture.

Over should not be used for *more than* to express an excess of an
amount or a number.

Example: His salary will be more than (not *over*) $10,000.

Overdo means to do something excessively.
  Overdue *means past due.*

Examples: Try not to overdo this summer.
            His July payment is overdue.

Overly should not be used for *over.*

Example: The members of the team were overconfident (not
            overly confident) before the game.

Packed means put in a container.
  Pact means treaty.

Examples: Your order should be packed today.
            When was the pact signed?

Paid means to give remuneration.
  Payed means to coat with pitch.

Examples: He paid his bill on time.
            The sailors payed the hull of the ship.

Pail is a container.
  Pale means dim.
  Pall is a cloth draped on a casket.

Examples: He poured a pail of water on the tree.

His new car is pale blue.
The pall was removed after the service.

Pair means two similar items.
  Pare means to peel.
  Pear is a fruit.

  Examples: You should buy a new pair of gloves.
              Pare the apple before you eat it.
              The pear tree has lots of fruit on it this year.

Pairs is the plural of the noun *pair*.
  Sets is the plural of the noun *set*.

  Examples: She bought five pairs (not *pair*) of gloves.
              She has three sets of dishes.
              He has one set of golf clubs.

Pale — See *Pail*.
Pall — See *Pail*.
Parcel is a package.
  Partial means inclined to favor or a part of the whole.

  Examples: Send the box by parcel post.
              That parcel should be mailed today.
              The boss was partial to blonde secretaries.
              Only a partial shipment was made.

Pardon — See *Excuse*.
Pare — See *Pair*.
Part — See *Percentage*.
Partial — See *Parcel*.
Partially means inclined to favor one person more than another.
  Partly means in some measure or in some part.

  Examples: He was treated partially by the supervisor.
              She was partly to blame.

Party is correctly used for *person* only in legal papers.

  Example: Mr. Lewis is the person (not *party*) who waited
              on you.

Passed is the past tense of *pass*.
  Past is an adjective or a noun. (See *Last*.)

  Examples: He passed my desk as he went to his office.
              In the past he has been punctual.
              His payments are past due.

Patience is an act of being patient.
  Patients are people receiving services.

Examples: Much patience is necessary to complete this task
            successfully.
            The doctor calls on many patients at their homes.

Patient — See *Client.*
Patients — See *Patience.*
Patron — See *Client.*
Payed — See *Paid.*
Peace means quietness or freedom from strife.
  Piece means portion.

Examples: Many people do not have peace of mind.
            His dessert was a piece of cake.

Pear — See *Pair.*
Pedal is a lever operated by a foot.
  Peddle means to sell or to distribute.

Examples: The piano pedal needs repairing.
            He peddles magazines.

Peer means to look with curiosity or a person of the same level as
another.
  Pier is a pillar or a landing place for a boat.

Examples: Nathan peered through the crack in the wall.
            The soldier was condemned by his peers.
            The boat approached the pier slowly.

People — See *Persons.*
Per should be used only with other Latin words, such as *per diem* and
per capita, and should not be used for *a* or *an*.

Examples: What is his per diem allowance?
            He types 60 words a minute (not *per minute*).
            His expenses were $8 a day (not *per day*).

Percentage is incorrectly used for *part* or *portion*.

Example: That city has hot weather a large part (not
            percentage) of the time.

Percept is an impression.
  Precept is an order or a rule.

Examples: Concepts are formed from percepts in a person's
            environment.
            He considered the precepts of his predecessors in
            forming his policies.

Perpetrate means to perform or carry out.
  Perpetuate means to make last indefinitely.

Examples: They perpetrated the deed as they had planned.
That endowment will perpetuate the work of the benevolent society.

Perquisite is a gratuity.
Prerequisite is something that must be done before something else can be done.

Examples: They left a large perquisite to express their appreciation.
What is the prerequisite for calculus?

Persecute means to cause suffering.
Prosecute means to bring legal proceedings against a person.

Examples: People have often been persecuted because of their beliefs.
He was prosecuted for the crime.

Person — See *Party*.
Personal is an adjective.
Personnel is a noun.

Examples: Please give the letter your personal attention.
The personnel of that business is very dependable.

Persons expresses individuality.
People expresses collection.
Individual expresses a person in particular but is seldom used except as an adjective.

Examples: All persons who arrive before noon will get free tickets.
Many people attended the performance.
As an individual, you have inalienable rights.

Perspective means true or proper relationship or outlook.
Prospective refers to a prospect or something expected.

Examples: Observing the parts in perspective was difficult.
From what perspective are you viewing this situation?
Five prospective candidates are being considered.

Peruse means to read.
Pursue means to follow.

Examples: Will you please peruse this material I have written?
Do you pursue a certain schedule in doing your work?

Phase — See *Faze*.

Phenomena — See *Data.*
Physical — See *Fiscal.*
Piece — See *Peace.*
Pier — See *Peer.*
Plain means ordinary, simple, or level country.
   Plane is a flat surface or an aircraft.

      Examples: How long was taken crossing the plains of
                   Nebraska?
                The surface of the plane is smooth.

Plaintiff is one who files a lawsuit.
   Plaintive means melancholy.

      Examples: The plaintiff filed his claim in January.
                The plaintive howling of coyotes pierced the
                   midnight air.

Plane — See *Plain.*
Pleas are appeals for mercy or assistance.
   Please means to make pleasant or to give pleasure. (See *Kindly*.)

      Examples: Their pleas for help were not heard.
                The decision pleased the chairman.

Plurality — See *Majority.*
Poorly is incorrectly used for *poor health.*

      Example: His employer is in poor health (not *poorly*).

Populace means a group of people.
   Populous means crowded.

      Examples: The populace shouted during the demonstration.
                Do you live in a populous area?

Portend means to give some sign of the future.
   Pretend means to profess. *Like* should not be used after *pretend.*

      Examples: What does this action portend?
                Ruby pretended (not *pretended like*) she could not
                   hear his instructions.

Portion — See *Percentage.*
Postal card is a card printed by the United States Government.
   Postcard is a mailing card printed by a private printer.

      Examples: Buy a dozen postal cards at the post office.
                While you are at the drugstore, buy two picture
                   postcards.

Posted should not be used for *mailed.* (See *Informed.*)

Examples: The secretary mailed the letter at 4:30.
             The letter was postmarked p.m.

Practicable means feasible.
  Practical means useful.

Examples: This solution seems practicable.
             Are these ideas practical?

Practically should not be used for *almost*.

Example: The swimmers were almost (not *practically*)
            drowned.

Pray means implore.
  Prey is a helpless animal or person.

Examples: The men on the raft prayed to be rescued.
             The hunters found their prey difficult to locate.

Precede means to be, go, or come before.
  Proceed means to move onward.

Examples: The band will precede the floats in the parade.
             How soon can you proceed with the project?

Precedence means preceding in time or priority.
  Precedent means an example.

Examples: The first order takes precedence over the second.
             This action may set a precedent.

Precept — See *Percept.*
Preposition is a part of speech.
  Proposition is a proposal. *Proposition* is not a verb except in im-
  polite company.

Examples: How many prepositions did he use to end the
                 sentence?
             His propositon was readily accepted.

Prerequisite — See *Perquisite.*
Prescribe means designate or specify.
  Proscribe means prohibit.
  Subscribe means to sign one's name or to support.

Examples: The doctor will prescribe the proper medicine.
             As proscribed by law, we cannot take this action.
             We subscribe to the objectives of the
                 organization.

Presence is the act of being present.
  Presents are gifts.

Examples: Can you prove your presence there on that date?
             The children received many presents.

Pretend — See *Portend.*
Prey — See *Pray.*
Price — See *Figure.*
Principal is usually an adjective; however, it is a noun when it means
   the chief person, the main items, or a capital sum.
   Principle is always a noun and means rule.

Examples: He met the principal of the school.
             What are the principal duties in his new job?
             What rate of interest do you pay on the principal?
             Learn the principles outlined in the lecture.

Probably — See *Likely.*
Proceed — See *Precede.*
Profit is gain.
   Prophet is one who predicts the future.

Examples: How much profit did he make on the transaction?
             Prophets foretold many miracles.

Prophecy is a noun meaning prediction.
   Prophesy is a verb meaning to predict.

Examples: Did the prophecy come true?
             What did he prophesy would happen?

Proportion — See *Apportion.*
Propose means to offer for consideration.
   Purpose means intent or objective.

Examples: What solution did he propose for the problem?
             I cannot understand what his purpose was in doing
                that.

Proposition — See *Preposition.*
Proscribe — See *Prescribe.*
Prosecute — See *Persecute.*
Prospective — See *Perspective.*
Proved is the preferred past tense of *prove. Proven* is the adjective
   form.

Examples: The problem has been proved many times.
             This is a proven fact.

Provided means on condition or if.
   Providing means supplying or furnishing.

Examples: I shall be there provided I can start the car.

They have been providing him with necessities.
The law providing for capital punishment was
abolished.

Purpose — See *Propose*.
Pursue — See *Peruse*.
Quay — See *Key*.
Quire — See *Choir*.
Quorum — See *Majority*.
Raise means to lift. (See *Rise*, p. 70.)
  Rays are beams of light.
  Raze means to demolish.

Examples: Please raise the window.
            The rays of the sun are streaming in the window.
            After they raze the old buildings, new ones will be
            built.

Raise refers to the growing of animals, fowls, and crops.
  Rear refers to the upbringing of children.

Examples: Every year that family raises many chickens.
            How many children did that family rear?

Rap means to knock.
  Wrap means to envelop.

Examples: Rap on the door before you enter the office.
            Wrap the package in heavy paper before you mail
            it.

Rather — See *Sooner*.
Ravaging means destructive.
  Ravenous refers to a strong urge for food or gratification.
  Ravishing means unusually attractive.

Examples: The ravaging winds ruined the campsite.
            He has a ravenous desire for fame.
            The blonde was ravishing.

Rays — See *Raise*.
Raze — See *Raise*.
Real should not be used for *very* or *really*.

Examples: This is a very (not *real*) good job.
            The cake was really (not *real*) good.

Reality is something that actually exists.
  Realty is real estate.

    Examples: His dream became a reality.
                   Does he deal in realty?

Rear — See *Raise.*
Reason — See *Excuse.*
Receipt is an acknowledgment of having received money or goods.
   Recipe is a set of directions or a formula.

    Examples: Did you give him a receipt for his payment?
                   The recipe makes six servings.

Recent refers to time that passed a short time ago.
   Resent means to feel displeasure.

    Examples: The recent rain was beneficial.
                   He resented the attitude that Mr. Randall had.

Recipe — See *Receipt.*
Reckon — See *Calculate.*
Reference means referral.
   Reverence is honor or respect.

    Examples: What reference did he make to the book?
                   All of his acts displayed reverence.

Refute means to disprove.
   Repute refers to reputation.

    Examples: Because of his evidence, we were unable to refute
                   his argument.
                   The First National Bank was reputed to be the
                   most substantial bank in the city.

Regardless — See *Irregardless.*
Relations should not be used for *relatives.*

    Example: My relatives (not *relations*) live in Missouri.

Remainder — See *Balance.*
Replica — See *Copy.*
Reprieve is a temporary delay of a penalty.
   Reprise is a repetition.

    Examples: The criminal was given a reprieve.
                   The reprise came in the second act of the
                   musical.

Reputation — See *Character.*
Repute — See *Refute.*
Resent — See *Recent.*
Residence means a place of abode.

Residents are the people who live in a place.

Examples: What is the address of his residence?
How many residents are in that house?

Respectfully means courteously.
Respectively means in the following order.

Examples: He answered respectfully.
Jones, Smith, and Brown were president, secretary, and treasurer, respectively, of their company.

Rest — See *Balance.*
Reverence — See *Reference.*
Right means correct.
Rite is a ceremony.
Wright is a carpenter.
Write means to record letters or words.

Examples: The solution to the problem was almost right.
The religious rite was impressive.
The wright did a beautiful piece of work.
Write to the director for his approval.

Rise — See *Rise*, p. 70.
Risky means hazardous.
Risque means verging on indecency.

Examples: Making that trip on ice is risky.
The performance was rather risque!

Rite — See *Right.*
Role means a function or a part played by an actor or an actress.
Roll means a cylindrical bundle, a pastry, a list, and to revolve.

Examples: Elizabeth Taylor played the role of Cleopatra.
The president has an important role in the company.
He carried a roll of money in his pocket.
We ate rolls and drank coffee.
Roll the barrels down the hill.

Roomer is one who rents a room.
Rumor is hearsay.

Examples: The roomer leaves early for work.
Who began such a terrible rumor?

Root is the part of a plant that grows in the ground.
Rout means to throw into confused flight.
Route is a course of way to be traveled or an assigned territory.

Examples: The plant died because its main root was cut.
            The enemy was routed at dawn.
            That mail route is a very long one.

Rumor — See *Roomer.*
Run should not be used to mean operate or manage a business.

Example: They operate (not *run*) a grocery store.

Sail means to travel on water.
  Sale is the selling of merchandise or services.

Examples: The Queen Mary will sail Tuesday.
            Our store will start its big sale on August 1.

Salary — See *Fee.*
Sale — See *Sail.*
Salvage means to save.
  Selvage is the edge of material that will not ravel.

Examples: Only a few items were salvaged after the fire.
            Place this side of the pattern toward the selvage.

Same is an adjective and should not be used as a pronoun.

Example: He returned the book (not *returned same*) to me.

Scent — See *Cent.*
Sealing — See *Ceiling.*
Secede means to withdraw.
  Succeed means to be successful.

Examples: They seceded from the organization.
            Mr. Morrow seems to succeed in convincing others
            he is right.

Seize means to grasp.
  Siege is an attack.

Examples: Seize the opportunity to get the position while you
            can.
            The siege of flu was worse in January than in
            February.

Selvage — See *Salvage.*
Semimonthly means twice a month.
  Semiweekly means twice a week.

Examples: That committee meets semimonthly. (Twice a
            month)
            The paper is published semiweekly. (Twice a week)
            (To avoid misunderstanding, use *twice monthly*
            and *twice weekly.)*

Senses — See *Censure*.

Sent — See *Cent*.

Serge is a type of fabric.

　Surge means to rise and fall like waves of water.

    Examples:　Mr. Marsh has a new serge suit.

              The waves of water surged eight feet high.

Serial — See *Cereal*.

Session — See *Cession*.

Settle — See *Locate*.

Sets — See *Pairs and* "Verbs" in "Grammar Problems," p. 69.

Shall — See *Shall*, p. 70.

Shape — See *Condition*.

Shear means to cut.

　Sheer means thin or steep.

    Examples:　When you finish mowing the lawn, shear the hedge.

              The curtains are made of sheer material.

Should — See Shall, p. 70.

Siege — See *Seize*.

Sight — See *Cite*.

Sit — See *Sit*, p. 69.

Site — See *Cite*.

Size is not an adjective and should not be used for *sized*.

    Example:　They moved into a small-sized (not *small-size*)
             house.

Sleight means crafty.

　Slight means to neglect.

    Examples:　The magician did unusual sleight-of-hand tricks.

              The employees frequently slight the work they
              dislike.

Some — See *Somewhat*.

Some one is an adjective modifying a noun and means some specific
　but unknown thing or person. *Some* is usually unnecessary.

　Someone is a personal pronoun and means somebody.

    Examples:　Some one of the items will be used.

             Someone will meet you at the terminal.

Some time is the noun modified by the adjective *some*. If *little* can
　be put between *some* and *time*, two words should be used.

　Sometime is an adverb and means at no definite or specified time.

    Examples:　Some time has passed since you made that trip.

             The mail arrived some time ago.

             Come to·visit us sometime.

Someone — See *Some one.*
Somewhat is an adverb, but *some* is an adjective.

> Examples: His father is somewhat (not *some*) better than he
>   was last week.
>   We bought some stationery.

Sooner should not be used for *rather.*

> Example: I'd rather (not *sooner*) arrive at the meeting early.

Sort of — See *Kind of.*
Specie is a kind of money.
   Species is a class or a category.

> Examples: What specie of money did you find?
>   He collected many species of butterflies.

Stake is a piece of wood standing up in the ground.
   Stakes are amounts of money or prizes.
   Steak is a slice of meat.

> Examples: Those stakes mark the location of the new building.
>   The stakes at the races were high.
>   How do you like steak cooked?

Stationary is an adjective. (Stationary means stand.)
   Stationery is a noun. (Stationery means paper for a letter.)

> Examples: A stationary table will be needed for that work.
>   Her friend gave her a box of stationery.

Statue is the likeness of a person or a thing.
   Stature refers to height or eminence.
   Statute is a law.

> Examples: A statue was erected in his honor.
>   He is a man of great stature.
>   This statute prohibits such action.

Stayed — See *Stopped.*
Steak — See *Stake.*
Stile is a set of steps for climbing over a wall or a fence.
   Style means fashion.

> Examples: He climbed the stile to retrieve his golf ball.
>   This is the latest style in suit coats.

Stopped should not be used for *stayed.*

> Example: We stayed (not *stopped*) overnight at the motel.

Straight means without bends or curves.

Strait is a narrow passage between two bodies of water.

Examples: The highway is straight between those two towns.
We passed through the strait at night.

Strata — See *Data.*
Style — See *Stile.*
Subscribe — See *Prescribe.*
Succeed — See *Secede.*
Suit is two- or three-piece wearing apparel.
  Suite is a set of rooms or furniture for a room.
  Sweet is the opposite of sour.

Examples: Mr. Baldwin is the man wearing the light gray suit.
Mr. Powell plans to purchase a new living-room
suite.
The sauce is not sweet enough.

Superintendence is supervision.
  Superintendents are executives.

Examples: Superintendence in the plant is strong.
All superintendents are interested in such an
improvement.

Suppose — See *Anticipate* and *Calculate.*
Sure emphasizes the state of assurance.
  Surely is an adverb meaning securely or undoubtedly.

Examples: He will be sure to do what you instruct him to do.
He surely did well on the test.

Surge — See *Serge.*
Suspect is a verb meaning to have doubts or to distrusts.
  Suspect can also be a noun meaning one who is suspected.
  Suspicion is a noun meaning the act of suspecting.

Examples: Harry suspected that the truth had not been told.
One does not "suspicion" a person; one suspects
him.
Her suspicions about his actions were correct.

Sweet — See *Suite.*
Symbol — See *Cymbal.*
Tail is the end piece.
  Tale is a story.

Examples: Our white cat has a black tail.
Who started such a tale?

Tares are the amounts deducted for containers when weighing material.

Tears means pulls apart.

Tiers are rows.

    Examples: How much weight was allowed for tares?
                  This material tears easily.
                  This chorus is arranged in four tiers.

Teach — See *Learn.*

Tears — See *Tares.*

Telegram — See *Wire.*

Than is used in comparisons.

   Then refers to time and means therefore.

    Examples: This machine is newer than that machine.
                  If this is true, then that is false.
                  Then was a good time to go.

That — See *That*, p. 67).

That there and *this here* should not be used where *this* and *that* are sufficient.

    Examples: This (not *this here*) typewriter needs repairing.
                  He repaired that (not *that there*) typewriter.
                  Lay that there and lay this here.

The — See *A.*

Their is a possessive pronoun.

   There means at that point or place.

   They're is the contraction for *they are.*

    Examples: All members found their names on the list.
                  Sign your name there.
                  They're ready to go.

Then — See *Than.*

Therefor means in return for something.

   Therefore means consequently.

    Examples: He sent a check in payment therefor.
                  He was late; therefore, he called a taxicab.

They're — See *There.*

This here — See *That there.*

Thorough means detailed or complete.

   Threw is the past tense of *Throw.*

   Through means from one point to another or finished.

    Examples: Henry made a thorough examination of the
                      situation.

The secretary threw away the rough-draft copy of
the letter.

The tour through the building will be at 2 p.m.

Throughout — See *Around.*
Tiers — See *Tares.*
Til means sesame.
  'til is the contraction of *until.*
  Till means until, a cash drawer, or a plow.

  Examples: Til is an herb or the seed of the herb.
  Wait 'til the train arrives.
  Don't go till I see you.

To is a preposition or a part of an infinitive. (See *On.*)
  Too is an adverb and means also or extent.
  Two is a number.

  Examples: She rode the train to Denver.
  We plan to open a new store in Chicago.
  The sun is too hot for you to work outside.
  Ronald plans to go too.
  Jim has two cars.

Topography refers to the features of land.
  Typography is the appearance of printing.

  Examples: The topography of that section of the state is
  rough.
  The typography of the manual is attractive.

Tortuous means crooked, winding, or involved.
  Torturous means with torture.

  Examples: We followed a tortuous path up the mountain.
  His injuries were torturous.

Toward is the preferred American usage. *Towards* is British usage.

  Example: We walked toward the building.

Track is a trace of a wheel or a foot.
  Tract is an area of land.

  Examples: A track was found in the mud outside the
  building.
  Mr. Wilson purchased a large tract of land for
  a shopping center.

Trail means path.
  Trial is an attempt.

Examples: Follow the trail to the cabin.

Numerous trials were made before a successful method was found.

Transparent — See *Opaque.*
Trial — See *Trail.*
Typography — See *Topography.*
Uninterested — See *Disinterested.*
Unless — See *Without.*
Unorganized — See *Disorganized.*
Until — See *Til.*
Usually — See *Generally.*
Vain means conceited or not successful.
   Vane is an object showing wind direction.
   Vein is a blood vessel or a style.

Examples: All of his efforts so far have been in vain.

The weather vane indicates that the wind is in the north.

The broken jar severed a vein in her finger.

The speaker spoke in a humorous vein.

Veracity means truthfulness.
   Voracity is the state of being extremely hungry.

Examples: His veracity was never questioned.

The children's voracity was noticed by all present.

Vice means wickedness; or, as a prefix, *vice* means taking the place of or next below.
   Vise is an instrument for holding objects.

Examples: Detective Noe heads the vice squad.

Mr. Green is the vice-president.

Put the rod in the vise to hold it steady.

Vocation — See *Avocation.*
Voracity — See *Veracity.*
Wage — See *Fee.*
Waist is the part of the body between the chest and the hips.
   Waste means something not used or not used efficiently.

Examples: What is Margaret's waist measurement?

This task is a waste of time.

Waive means to postpone or to refrain from enforcing.
   Wave is a sweep of the hand or a loose movement.

Examples: The attendance requirement was waived for the student.

The lad waved as the train departed.
That ocean wave was huge.

Waiver is the giving up of a claim or a privilege.
   Waver means to fluctuate.

     Examples: He signed a waiver on the property.
                Frequently Sam wavered when he attempted to
                make a decision.

Ware is an item of merchandise.
   Wear means to have on the body or to use.

     Examples: Many merchants display their wares on sidewalks.
                This type of carpet will not wear well in the
                lobby.
                What dress are you going to wear to the meeting?

Waste — See *Waist*.
Wave — See *Waive*.
Waver — See *Waiver*.
Way instead of *ways* should be used when referring to distance.

     Examples: He went a long way to get the car.
                He was quite a way (not *ways*) ahead of us.

Weak is an adjective meaning not strong.
   Week is a noun specifying seven successive days.

     Example: He broke his weak ankle last week.

Wear — See *Ware*.
Weather refers to atmospheric conditions.
   Whether is a conjunction and refers to alternatives.

     Examples: The weather should be pleasant for the picnic
                today.
                He couldn't decide whether to buy a machine or to
                rent one.

Well — See *Good*.
Whether — See *If* and *Weather*.
Which — See *That* and *Which*, p. 67.
Whole — See *Hole*.
Wholly — See *Holey*.
Who's is a contraction of *who is*.
   Whose is a possessive pronoun.

       Examples: Who's coming?
                  Whose secretary is she?

Will — See *Will*, p. 70.

Wire should not be used for *telegram* or *telegraph*.

> Examples: When did you receive the telegram (not *the wire*)?
> When did you telegraph (not *wire*) him?

Without should not be used for *unless*. *Without* is followed by nouns, and *unless* is followed by phrases.

> Examples: I shall not go unless the president approves the trip.
> I shall not go without the president's approval.

Would — See *Will*, p. 70.

Wrap — See *Rap*.

Wright — See *Right*.

Write — See *Right* and *Contact*.

Your is a possessive pronoun.

You're is a contraction of *you are*.

> Examples: Your call came at an opportune time.
> You're expected to be present at the meeting.

Yourself — See *Herself*.

Writing, as well as conversation, can become filled with meaningless cliches and trite expressions. Business correspondence is especially notorious for the preservation of hackneyed, stilted, redundant, and vague expressions. Many of these expressions are carryovers from formal conversation and writing of the 18th and 19th centuries and have long ago lost their appropriateness.

Modern writing should be clear, concise, straightforward, and precise. Although society has not accepted everyday conversation as proper writing, modern writing favors an informal tone and a conversational style. In choosing words and expressions to write, a good rule to follow is *don't write something you wouldn't carefully say.* However, just because you would say something doesn't necessarily mean that you should write it. After all, once you have written something, you have lost the privilege of changing your words to prevent or to lessen your embarrassment of having said something inappropriately.

The following pages contain many trite, wordy, antiquated, and redundant expressions that should be eliminated from modern writing. These expressions are listed in the left column; suggested expressions and comments for improvement are listed in the right column.

Trite Expressions	Suggested Improvements
absolutely complete	complete
a common belief of many people	a common belief
accept of	accept
according to our records	(Be direct. Everyone gets information from records.) your account is ten days past due
acknowledge receipt of acknowledge with pleasure acknowledging your letter of July 1	thank you for your letter
advised and informed	advised (or) informed (not both)
agreeable and satisfactory	agreeable (or) satisfactory (not both)

agreeable to your request	as you requested
all kinds of	all
all the further (or) farther	as far as
allow me to	may I
along the lines of along these lines	like
also . . . too (they also want that too)	also (or) too (not both)
amount up to	amount to
an entire monopoly of the whole market	a monopoly
answer in the affirmative	answer *yes* (or) answer affirmatively
anywhere near	not nearly
and etc.	and so forth (or) etc. (But try to eliminate the expression.)
anticipate	expect
anticipate ahead	anticipate (or) expect
anxious and eager	anxious (or) eager
aren't I	am I not
as a matter of fact	(Five superfluous words)
as captioned above as stated above as stated below	(Avoid repetition if possible.) as I said as mentioned on page two as will be explained
as otherwise	as
as per as per your order	according to according to your order
as regards	regarding
as the case may be	(Five superfluous words)
as to	(Avoid the expression.)
as yet we have not heard	we have not heard
ascend up to	ascend
ask the question	ask
assemble together with	assemble (or) assemble with
assuring you of our prompt attention	(Be specific. Tell what you will do when.)
as soon as possible at an early date at the earliest possible moment	(Be specific. Say when.)

at 4 p.m. in the afternoon	at 4 p.m.
at about at around	(One preposition is enough.)
at all times	always
at hand	(Two unnecessary words; trite expression)
at some point of time	at some time
at the present writing at this time	now
at your earliest convenience	at your convenience (Or be specific and say when.)
attached find attached hereto, herewith, please find	attached is (*Find* connotes a search.)
autobiography of his life	autobiography (or) his autobiography
avail yourself of this opportunity	(18th century expression)
awaiting your favor awaiting your further orders awaiting your further reply	(Be specific. Ask for a reply by a certain time.)
bank on	rely on
basic fundamentals	(Redundancy. Fundamentals are basic.)
beg to acknowledge beg to advise beg to announce beg to assure beg to call beg to confirm beg to inform	(Only beggars beg.)
being that	since, because, (or) as
biographies of the lives of great men	biographies of great men
blame it on him blame on	blame him blame (or) blamed
both alike both also both as well as both equally both of these both together	(Redundancies. Use only *both* or eliminate *both.*)
but however	but (or) however (not both)

buy up	buy
by means of	by
by return mail	(No such mail service is provided!)
call up	call (or) telephone
carbon copy of	carbon of (or) copy of
careful consideration	consideration
carefully noted	noted
check into check over	check
check to cover	check for
check up on	check on
circular in form	circular
combined together with	combined (or) combined with
command (awaiting your further command)	(For the militia and slaves only.)
complete monopoly	monopoly
complying with your letter of complying with your request	(Be specific. Tell what you will do.)
conclude at the end	conclude
connect up with	connect (or) connect with
connected with a company	member of a company
consensus of opinion	consensus
consider as consider him as a prospect	consider consider him a prospect
contact	call, phone, see, (or) write
contemplate on (or) over	think about (or) consider
contents duly noted	(A snide expression)
continue on	continue
continue to remain	continue (or) remain
count on	depend on
courteous and polite	courteous (or) polite (not both)
customary practice	customary (or) practice (not both)
date of August 1	August 1 (The reader will recognize a date as such.)
dates back to	dates from
deduct a discount of 6 percent	deduct 6 percent
deeds and actions	deeds (or) actions (not both)

demand and insist	demand (or) insist (not both)
depreciate in value	depreciate
desire to state	(Go ahead and say it.)
despite the fact that	despite
disseminate	spread
do not use the word *formalize*	("the word" is unnecessary)
don't ever	never
doubt but	doubt
due course	(Be specific.)
due to the fact that	because (or) due to
duly	(Eliminate *duly*.)
duly credited duly entered duly noted	
during the course of during the years 1970-1974	during from 1970 through 1974
each and every	each (or) every (not both)
each in its respective way	in their respective ways
either this or else that	either this or that
else but	else
enclosed herewith enclosed please find	enclosed (*Find* connotes a search.)
end up in	end in
endorse on the back	endorse
enlarge in size	enlarge
entirely complete	complete
equally as big as equally as good as	as big as (or) as large as as good as
every bit as	just as
every so often	occasionally, frequently, (or) seldom
exactly identical	identical
extra special	special
fall off of the wagon	fall off the wagon
favor	(An ancient substitute for *letter* or *order*.)
few and far between	few, scarce, (or) rare
final completion	completion

finish off finish up	finish, end, (or) complete
first and foremost	first (or) foremost (not both)
first before	first (or) before
first began first begin	began begin
fold up	fold
folks	relatives
follows after	follows (or) after (not both)
for some time now	for two weeks since January 1 (Be specific.)
for the purpose of for the reason that	for
formalize	(Do not use.)
forward (or) forwarded	sent (or) send
free gratis	free
full and complete	complete (or) full (not both)
furnished on request	as you requested
generally known by most people	generally known
give attention to	(Be specific. Tell what kind of attention you want.)
give out	give
goals and objectives	goals (or) objectives (not both)
go back to New York (a first visit)	go to New York
goes on to say	says, adds, (or) continues
going on	approaching
gone forward	gone
greatly minimize	minimize
guess	think (or) believe (OK if you mean guess.)
hand you herewith	enclosed is
has come to hand	(Ancient, ridiculous expression)
have before us	have
heard of this	heard this
help but help from	help
hereby advise	advise

hereby hesitate	hesitate
herewith enclose	enclosed is
herewith find	
herewith please find	
hoping for your favor	(Hackneyed expressions)
hoping for your order	
hoping to receive	
I, myself; he, himself	I, he (needless repetition)
I am	(Modern correspondents omit
I remain	these ancient expressions be-
	fore complimentary closes.)
I cannot but help hoping	I cannot help hoping
I have received your report	(Wasted words. If you answer or
I have your letter before me	comment on his letter or
I have your letter of June 1	report, the reader will know
	you have it.)
I trust	I hope (Antiquated expression)
immediately and at once	immediately (or) at once
important essentials	essentials
in a precise manner	precisely (or) with precision
in accordance with your request	as you requested (or) as you
	wished
in answer to same	(Be more subtle. Your correspon-
in answer to yours	dent will recognize your
	answer to his letter.)
in any way, shape, or form	in any way
in conclusion I would state	(Go ahead and say it.)
in conformance with your request	as you requested (or) as you
	wished
in connection therewith	in connection with
in disregard of	disregarding
in due course	(Be specific. When?)
in due course of time	
in lieu of	in place of (or) for
in order that	so that (or) to
in order to	
in other words	(Say it clearly the first time so
	you won't have to repeat.)
in re	regarding (Avoid Latin
	expressions.)
in receipt of	I received

in reference to	regarding
in reply to your favor in reply wish to state in reply would advise in reply would wish in response to your in response to your favor	(Good enough for your grand- father but not good enough for you. Be direct.)
in the amount of	for
in the event that	should
in the French language	in French
in the last analysis	(Ridiculous unless you have made several analyses! What about the first analysis?)
in the manner of	as (or) like
in the midst of	among, within, (or) throughout
in the nature of	like
in the near future	soon, tomorrow, next week, (or) on July 1 (Be specific. When?)
in the neighborhood of	about (or) nearly
in the normal course	(Be specific. When?)
in this connection	(Usually three unnecessary words)
in this day and age	today
in this matter	(Be specific. What is the matter?)
in view of the fact that	in view of
inasmuch as	because (or) since
incorporate	include
inform	tell
initial beginning	beginning
inquire	ask
inside of	within
it is in the shape of a square	it is square
it is made in such a manner as to give	it is made to give
-ize, -ized	(Avoid stilted words such as *finalize*, especially homemade *ize* words.)
joint partnership, co-partnership	partnership (An equal partnership refers to equal distribution of earnings and not necessarily equal division of assets.)

just perfect	perfect
just recently	recently
kind indulgence kind letter kind order	(Omit *kind* unless you mean sympathetic.)
kind of, sort of	(OK if you mean variety)
kind of a	kind of
kindly advise kindly confirm kindly send	please tell please confirm please send
larger in size	larger

let me call your attention to
may I call your attention to
	(Why ask permission to do some-
	    thing you will do without
	    permission?)

lift up	lift (Lift down?)
like for	like
loosen up	loosen
lose out	miss (or) lose
lots lots of	much, many, (or) a great deal
lower left-hand corner	lower-left corner
made out of	made of
made the statement that	said that
many excellent benefits	many benefits
many in number	many
may or may not may perhaps	may

may we hope to receive
may we suggest
	(Again, why ask permission for
	    something you will do without
	    permission?)

more difficult	harder
narrate	tell
near to	near
necessary essentials (requirements)	essentials (requirements)
necessity	this is necessary
never yet	never
new innovation	innovation
no good	worthless
not as yet	not yet

nothing else but	nothing but
nowhere near	not nearly
of above date	(Be specific. Give the exact date.)
of recent date	
of any sort or kind	of any sort (or) of any kind
off of	off
off of the	off the
often accustomed to	(Omit *often*.)
often in the habit of	
oftentimes	often
old adage	adage
on the grounds that	because of (Stilted)
on the occasion of	
on the part of	for (or) in behalf of
one and the same	the same
open up	open
opposite to	opposite
our records show	(Sounds as if you don't trust your records.)
outside of	outside
over with	over
pair of twins	twins
party (a party named Jones)	man (Let the lawyers use *party*.)
passed away	died
past experience	experience
pay out to	pay
per	(Latin again!)
permit me to say	(Asking permission?)
permit us to remind	
please accept	(Trite expressions)
please advise	
please find enclosed	
please find herewith	
please note	
please rest assured	
please return same	
please be advised that	(A ridiculous waste of four words)
please feel free	please

plenty good enough	good enough
posted	mailed (or) informed
pretend like	pretend that
previous to	before
prior to	before
pursuant to	according to
put in	spent
quite a few	several (or) many
ran into (a collision?)	met
rarely ever	rarely
re	(Latin!)
read where	read that
real	very
reason is because	(*Because*, *that*, and *why* are
reason that	superfluous.)
reason why	
recent date	(Be specific. Give the date.)
recent letter	
reduce to a minimum	minimize
refer back to (return, revert)	refer to (return to, revert to)
referring to the matter	(Be direct. The reader will
referring to your favor of	recognize references.)
referring to yours of	
refuse and decline	refuse (or) decline (not both)
regarding said order	(Trite expressions)
regarding the above	
regarding the matter	
regarding your letter	
regarding yours	
regret to advise	sorry that
regret to inform	
regret to state	
relations	relatives
relative to	regarding
repeat again	repeat
replying to yours of	(Hackneyed expression)
rest up	rest
right along	along
right and proper	right (or) proper (not both)

rise up	rise (Rise down?)
said (the said party)	(Let the lawyers use *said* as an adjective.)
same (as a pronoun)	(Let the lawyers use *same* as a pronoun.)
same identical	same (or) identical (not both)
saw where	saw that
see where	see that
seeing as how	because (or) since
seeing that	
seldom ever	seldom
	seldom if ever
	hardly ever
	scarcely ever
sending by mail	mailing
settle up the account	pay the account
shipping by express	shipping (or) expressing
shorter in height	shorter
show up	appear (or) arrive
size up	estimate, judge, evaluate, (or) appraise
small in size	small
small miniature	small (or) miniature
so as to	to
soliciting your advice	please tell me
square in form	square
start over again	begin again
state	say (or) tell
still remains	still (or) remains
subsequent to July 1	after July 1
surrounded on all sides by	surrounded by
take and put this in	put this in
take in	attend
take it under advisement	consider
take pleasure in	please to
take stock of	(Trite expressions)
take the liberty	
take this opportunity	
ten years ago since	ten years ago (or) since 1964

thank you again	(Once is enough.)
thank you kindly	thank you
thanking you in advance thanking you in anticipation	(Presumptuous to thank in advance)
thanking you, we remain	(Participial closings were all right in the past century.)
that alone is the reason	that is the reason (or) that is the only reason
that is to say	(Say it clearly the first time.)
the fact that	(Wasted words.)
the undersigned	I (or) me
the writer	(Don't use third person in business writing.)
This company of ours	our company
this is for the purpose of asking this is for the purpose of requesting this is to acknowledge this is to advise you	(Cliches! Be direct and avoid wordy expressions.)
this kind of a	this kind of
this will acknowledge receipt of your letter	thank you for your letter
thought and consideration	thought (or) consideration (not both)
to the right in a clockwise direction	to the right (or) clockwise
took sick	became ill
total effect of all this was to	total effect was
triangular form	triangular
true facts	facts
trust this will be satisfactory trusting to have trusting to receive	(Hackneyed expressions)
try out	try
under date of	dated
under separate cover	by parcel post
under the above subject	(Be precise. What subject?)
united in marriage	married
unjust and unfair	unjust (or) unfair (not both)
up above	above

up to	until
up to this writing	until today
up until	
upon investigation	on investigation
upon receiving your record	when we receive your record
upon reviewing our records	(Be direct and get to the point.)
valued (favor, order, business)	(Cliches of the 19th century)
very	(Very much overused)
very complete	complete
very large in size	large
very latest	latest
via	by (Use English.)
we are not in a position to	we cannot
we are of the opinion that	we believe
we are pleased to advise (to note)	we are glad to tell (to hear)
we do not deem it advisable	we do not believe (or) we believe it unwise
we have before us	(Your reader doesn't care what you have before you.)
we regret to inform you	we regret that
we take pleasure in advising	we are pleased that
we wish to say	(Asking permission?)
when first born	when born
where is it at	where is it
whether or not	whether
widow woman	widow (A widow is a woman.)
wire	telegram (or) telegraph
-wise	(Don't manufacture -*wise* words such as *percentagewise* and *temperaturewise*.)
with a view to	toward
with kindest regards	(Trite.)
with reference to	regarding
with regard to	
with relation to	
with respect to	
with the intention of	intending to
with the result that	resulting in
without further delay	without delay
witnessed	saw

would say, state, suggest, advise would wish to	(Stereotyped expressions)
write up	write
you claim you state	(Why tell the reader what he already knows?)
yours of the 15th received	(If you must refer to a specific letter, give the complete date of the letter.) thank you for your letter
your esteemed favor your esteemed order your favor has come to hand your future patronage your kind indulgence your letter of even date your letter of recent date	(Cliches from the 18th century)
your letter was duly received	thank you for your letter
your Mr. Jones	Mr. Jones of your company
yours (meaning your letter)	your letter
yours of the 15th received	thank you for your letter of June 15

An idiom, an expression peculiar to a language, cannot be explained by the definitions of the words used in the expression. Perhaps more than other parts of speech, prepositions combined with other words form the greatest number of idiomatic expressions in English.

The following list provides some idiomatic prepositional expressions. About the only explanation for their usage is that the vernacular of the language has given them certain meanings and has caused them to be used in certain ways.

Absolved	— absolved *by* a jury; absolved *of* or *from* guilt
Accede	— accede *to* a request
Accommodate	— accommodate a person *with* a loan; accommodate a person *by* lending him money; accommodate *to* an environment
Accompanied	— accompanied *by* (passive voice); accompanied *with* (active voice)
According	— according *to*
Account	— account *to* a person; account *for* a thing
Accountable	— accountable *to* a person; accountable *for* a thing
Accused	— accused *by* a person; accused *of* an act
Acquiesce	— acquiesce *in* an opinion
Acquit	— acquit *of* an offense; acquit *by* a jury
Adapt	— adapt *for* performance; adapt *to* a situation; adapt *from* a play or a book
Addicted	— addicted *to* a habit
Adequate	— adequate *for* (preposition meaning enough); adequate *to* (meaning equal to)
Admit	— admit *to* (not *in*) an organization
Advantage	— have advantage *over* something; of advantage *to* something; an advantage *in* something; gain or have an advantage *by* doing something; take advantage *of* something; the advantage *of* something is
Advise	— advise *with* people; advise *of* situations
Affinity	— affinity *between* or *among* things; affinity *for* something

Afflicted	— afflicted *with* a habit; afflicted *by* a disease or an injury
Agree	— agree *on* or *upon* ideas; agree *in* principle; agree *with* people; agree *to* act, *to* a plan
Agreeable	— agreeable *with* people; agreeable *to* a plan, *to* an idea
Analogous	— analogous *to* (not *with*)
Angry	— angry *about* or *at* an incident or a thing; angry *with* a person
Appeal	— appeal *against* a ruling; appeal *to* a court; *to* a person
Apply	— apply *to* a person; apply *for* a position, apply *at* a location
Apposition	— apposition *with*
Apprehensive	— apprehensive *of* peril; apprehensive *for* safety
Appropriate	— appropriate *for* a person; appropriate *to* an occasion
Argue	— argue *with* a person; argue *against* an idea; argue *about* a subject; argue *for* a proposition
Arrive	— arrive *in* a city or a town; arrive *at* a station, *at* a corner, *at* a site
Attempt	— attempt (noun) *at* a solution
Attested	— attested *to* (active voice); attested *by* (passive voice)
Aversion	— aversion *to* (not *for*)
Bathe	— bathe *with*(not *in*) water; bathe *in* a tub
Beneficial	— beneficial *to* (not *from*)
Bestow	— bestow *upon* (not *on*)
Bill	— bill *for* a debt or an account; bill *of* particulars or lading
Blame	— blame a person *for* something (not blame *on* a person)
Buy	— buy *from* (not *of*) a person or a company; buy *at* a store; buy *in* a city; buy *off* a cop; buy *out* a business (purchase an entire business); buy *out* a business (purchase a share of a business)
Care	— care *for* people or animals; care *about* appearance; careless *with* property; careless *in* performance
Cause	— cause *for* an action; cause *of* a result, *of* a sorrow
Center	— center *on* or *with* (not *around*)

Choice	— choice *of* things; choice *for* the position
Compare	— compare *to* an unlike item; compare *with* a similar item
Compatible	— compatible *with* (not *to*)
Complain	— complain *to* an individual; complain *about* or *of* things
Complementary	— complementary *to* (not *with*)
Compliance	— compliance *with* (not *to*)
Complimentary	— complimentary *to*
Comply	— comply *with* an order (fulfill a wish or a request)
Concur	— concur *with* a person or a thing; concur *in* an idea, *in* a decision, *in* an opinion
Conducive	— conducive *to* (not *of*) good health
Confer	— confer *on* (give to); confer *with* (talk with)
Confide	— confide *in* a person; confide an idea *to* a person
Conform	— conform *to* or *with* instructions (not *by*)
Connected	— connected *to* a pole; connected *by* a wire; connected *with* a company (trite)
Consequent	— consequent *to* (not *upon*)
Considerate	— considerate *of* (not *for*)
Consideration	— consideration *of* a situation; consideration *for* a person
Consist	— consist *of* many parts (not *with*)
Consult	— consult *with* people; consult a book; consulted *by* people
Contemporary	— contemporary *with* (not *to*)
Contend	— contend *with* or *against* crime; contend *for* improvements
Contrast	— contrast one item *with* another one; one thing is *in* contrast *to* another one
Convenient	— convenient *for* accomplishing a thing, *for* a person; convenient *to* a location
Converted	— converted *to* (not *over*)
Cooperate	— cooperate *in* doing things; cooperate *with* persons (not cooperate *together*)
Cooperation	— cooperation *in* doing things; cooperation *with* persons; (not cooperation *together*)
Correspond	— correspond *with* (write) a person; correspond *to* or *with* (comparison) an item
Cure	— cure *of* (not *from*)
Danger	— danger *in* something: danger *of* something happening
Dates	— dates *from* (not *back to*)
Deal	— deal *with* a person, *with* a problem; deal *in* technicalities and merchandise

Decline	— decline *from* a position; decline *of* the area; decline *in* reputation
Defect	— defect *in* (place); defect *of* (a type or kind)
Desirous	— desirous *of* success (not *for*)
Devoid	— devoid *of* (not *in*) humor
Die	— die *of* a disease; die *with* boots on, *with* others; die *for* a cause; die *from* exposure, *from* lack of care, *from* fatigue, *from* injuries; die *by* his own hand; die *in* bed, *in* a fire, *in* an accident; wind dies *down;* sounds die *away*
Differ	— differ *with* a person, *with* an opinion; differ *from* each other, *from* quantities; differ *about* an idea; differ *on* religious matters; differ *in* color, *in* opinion
Difference	— difference *of* opinion; difference *in* price; difference *between* two items; difference *among* several items
Difficulty	— difficulty *over* a plan; difficulty *about* or *in* making plans; difficulty *with* a problem
Disappointed	— disappointed *in* a situation, *in* a person; disappointed *by* what happened
Discrepancy	— discrepancy *in* an item; discrepancy *between* two items; discrepancy *among* several items
Dispense	— dispense *with* (not *of*)
Dispute	— dispute *over* or *about* regulations; dispute *with* a person; dispute *between* two people; dispute *among* several people
Dissension	— dissension *between* two people; dissension *among* several people; dissension *in* the ranks
Dissent	— dissent *from* the majority vote, *from* opinion; show dissent *by* speaking
Employed	— employed *for* a purpose; employed *at* an amount; employed *in* work, *in* a profession; employed *by* a person, *by* a company; employed *through* an agency
Enter	— enter *on* or *upon* a trip; enter *at* the door, *at* a point; enter *into* a contract, *into* a room; enter *upon* duties, *upon* a question; enter *in* a record
Exception	— exception *to* (not *from*); with the exception *of*
Experience	— experience *of* selling cars; experience *in* selling cars
Experienced	— experienced *in* selling cars
Familiar	— familiar *with* the situation, *with* employers; familiar *to* a person; looks familiar *to* me
Familiarize	— familiarize *with*

Fear	— fear *for* safety; fear *of* something; fear *in* a person, *in* a group
Foreign	— foreign *to* (not *from*)
Frightened	— frightened *by* something; frightened *at* the idea, *at* the thought; frightened *into* doing something; frightened *of* doing wrong
Furnished	— furnished *to* or *by* something; furnished *with* care, *with* chairs; furnished *in* a certain manner
Glad	— glad *for* a person; glad *of* or *for* your recovery
Grieve	— grieve *at, because of, over* or *about* your loss; grieve *for* a person
Grieved	— grieved *by* news
Guard	— guard *against* or *from* accidents; guard *by* men; guard *with* a gun
Happen	— happen *on* or *upon* a hill; happen *to* a person; happen *at* a time, *at* an intersection; happen *in* a building; happen *by* a place; happen *along* a trail
Hold	— hold *in* awe; hold *for* arrival; hold *together;* hold *on* to something; hold *down* a job; hold *out* an item; hold *off until* tomorrow; hold *over* the play; hold *up* a bank, *up* your hand; released his hold *on* the club; take hold *of* the knob; get hold *of* himself
Idea	— idea *about* or *on* a subject; idea *of* value; idea *for* you, *for* decorating
Identical	— identical *with* (not *to*) something
Ignorant	— ignorant *in* (uninformed); ignorant *of* (unaware)
Ill	— ill *with* (not *of*) a disease; ill *at* ease; spoke ill *of* them
Immune	— immune *to* a disease; immune *from* indebtedness; immune *for* a period of time
Impatient	— impatient *with* persons; impatient *with* or *about* things; impatient *at* the beginning, *at* the end; impatient *for* home
Imply	— imply *by* (not *in*) your actions
Incompatible	— incompatible *with* (not *to*)
Independent	— independent *of* (not *from*) another person; independent *for* a time; independent *about* a matter
Indifference	— indifference *about* two books; indifference *to* things; shows indifference *toward* things
Indifferent	— indifferent *to* (not *of*) things; indifferent *about* two books
Infer	— infer *from* (not *by*) your actions

Inferior — inferior *to* something; inferior *in* quality

Initiate — initiate *into* (not *in*) a club or an organization

Initiated — initiated *on* a date; initiated *at* a time, *at* a place; initiated *in* a building

Insensible — insensible *of* danger; insensible *to* or *from* fear, *to* or *from* pain; insensible *from* cold

Insensitive — insensitive *to* (not *from*) something

Intercede — intercede *with* a person; intercede *in* a matter; intercede *for* a person; intercede *in behalf of* someone

Interfere — interfere *with* a person, *with* a process; interfere *in* affairs

Invite — invite a person *to* dinner (not *for* dinner)

Join — join *in* activities, *in* marriage; join one item *to* another; join *with* a group

Jump — jump *to* or *at* conclusions; jump *into* water; jump *on* a bus; jump *up* and *down;* jump *upon* them; jump *off to* a good start; jump *out of* bed; jump *at* an opportunity; jump *from* here to there; jump *over* the fence; jump *without* thinking

Liable — liable *for* indebtedness; liable *to* a person you owe

Listen — listen *to* the siren; listen *for* a sound

Live — live *at* home; live *in* a home, *in* a city; live *with* people; live *on* a hill; live *for* a purpose

Means — means *of* paying; means *for* something; means *to* an end

Meet — meet *in* the building; meet *about* a matter; meet *for* a purpose; meet *over* coffee; meet *at* the corner; meet *with* people

Motive — motive *for* (not *in*)

Necessity — necessity *for* an event, *for* doing something; necessity *of* an obligation

Need — need *of* an item; need *for* an occasion

Oblivious — oblivious *of* (not *to*)

Opposite — opposite *of* (not *to*); opposite *in* opinion, *in* quality

Overcome — overcome *by* fumes; overcome *with* humiliation

Part — part *from* persons; part *with* things

Payment — payment *for* an article; payment *of* a price or bill

Permission — got permission *by* asking; got permission *from* the boss; got the permission *of* the boss

Proceed — proceed *to* a place; proceed *with* a matter, *with* caution

Profit — profit *by* doing something; profit *from* a sale; profit *in* a business; profit *of* a business

Provide	— provide *for* a person; provide *with* necessities; provide *against* loss
Purpose	— purpose *in* or *of* doing something (not *at*)
Quarrel	— quarrel *with* a person; quarrel *about* or *over* a matter; quarrel *to* extremes
Reason	— reason *with* a person; reason *about* a matter; reason *for* doing something
Recommend	— recommend *to* a person; recommend *by* letter; recommend *in* a letter
Reconcile	— reconcile *to* a situation; reconcile *with* a person; reconcile this *with* that
Recover	— recover *from* (not *of*) an illness; recover *within* a period of time; recover *in* time, *in* bed, *in* a hospital; recover *at* home; recover *during* prosperity; recover *for* a purpose
Rejoice	— rejoice *with* a person; rejoice *at* or *in* good luck
Represent(ed)	— represent *by* a person, *by* a symbol; represent *in* an illustration, *in* a meeting, *in* Congress; represent *as* true; represent *to* a group
Resentment	— resentment *against* or *toward* a person; resentment *at* or *for* an action
Retire	— retire *from* business; retire *with* a pension; retire *into* a room
Retroactive	— retroactive *to* (not *from*) a date
Right	— right *of* ownership; right *to* own
Sick	— sick *with* (not *from*) a disease
Stay	— stay *at* (not *to*) home; stay *in* a house; stay *with* a person; stay *on* the job; stay *for* a meeting
Subject	— subject *for* or *of* discussion; subject *to* a rule
Subscribe	— subscribe *to* an idea; subscribe *for* a magazine; subscribe *in* a year, *in* a month; subscribe *on* a date; subscribe *by* a specified time; subscribe *at* a place; subscribe *during* a period of time
Superior	— superior *to* (not *than* or *over*) something; superior *in* quality
Surround	— surround *by* objects; surround *with* people
Thirst	— thirst *for* or *after* knowledge; thirst *for* water
Trade	— trade *with* people; trade *in* merchandise; trade *at* a store; trade *for* an object
Turn	— turn *up* the heat to get warm; turn *down* the air conditioning to get cool
Vary	— vary *from* a plan; one item varies *from* another item (the items differ); one item varies *with* another item (the items move together) vary *in* this way

Wait   — wait *for* a person, *for* a train (*wait for* means delay
                    until); wait *on* a customer, *on* a sick person
                    (*wait on* means to serve)

Withheld   — withheld *from* a person; withheld *by* a person;
                    withheld *until* Saturday

INDEX